Fiber-optic systems

Fiber-optic systems

Network applications

Terry Edwards
Senior Research Analyst
Gosling Associates Technology Transfer Ltd,
Harrogate, UK

JOHN WILEY & SONS
Chichester · New York · Brisbane · Toronto · Singapore

Wiley Editorial Offices

John Wiley & Sons Ltd, Baffins Lane, Chichester,
West Sussex PO19 1UD, England.

John Wiley & Sons, Inc., 605 Third Avenue,
New York, NY 10158-0012, USA

Jacaranda Wiley Ltd, G.P.O. Box 859, Brisbane,
Queensland 4001, Australia.

John Wiley & Sons (Canada) Ltd, 22 Worcester Road,
Rexdale, Ontario M9W 1L1, Canada

John Wiley & Sons (SEA) Pte Ltd, 37 Jalan Pemimpin #05-04,
Block B, Union Industrial Building, Singapore 2057

Library of Congress Cataloging-in-Publication Data:

Edwards, T. C.   (Terence Charles)
     Fiber-optic systems : network applications   /
Terry Edwards.
          p.   cm.
     Includes index.
     ISBN 0 471 91567 X
     1. Fiber optics industry.   2. Fiber optics—Industrial
applications.   I. Title.
HD9696.F522E38   1989
338.4′ 76213692—dc20   89-14673
                                                                              CIP

British Library Cataloguing in Publication Data:

Edwards, T.C.
     Fiber-optic systems   :   network applications
     1. Telecommunication systems.   Applications
     of fibre optics
     I. Title
     621.38′ 0414

     ISBN 0 471 91567 X

Typeset by Mathematical Composition Setters Ltd, Salisbury, Wilts
Printed and bound in Great Britain by
Biddles Ltd, Guildford and King's Lynn

Contents

Preface: the fiber-optics market

Market analysts regularly publish USA and world projections and a general conclusion from most of these analysts is that in 1988 the total world market was around $2 billion (US) and that this is expected roughly to double by the early 1990s.

The markets for trunk telecommunications applications have leveled-off and even fallen in some countries and undersea (submarine) installations are projected to have an uneven monetary value of sales over the next 8 years. These undersea installations are expected to peak at about $1.5 billion in 1989, to remain at hundreds of million dollar values in the other years (actually negligible in 1994, but rising again later).

For the markets in the near future there are several influencing factors worth citing. In most major countries manufacturing over-capacity, which several observers consider may be as much as 30% for some (especially 'active') products, coupled with aggressive purchasing by big network operators such as PTTs, will force unit prices down. This will include primary coated fiber as volume production increases still further.

Overall, it is considered that unit prices of *all* products (except fiber and cable) will continue to fall until at least the early 1990s. Then the volume requirements are likely to level off as the trunk telecommunications installation rate falls. Continued market growth should be substainable by means of new opportunities in areas such as local area networks (LANs), metropolitan area networks (MANs), financial services networks, cable TV and military applications. These applications are all described in this book.

Also, products with further added-value are likely to appear (e.g. electro-optic modules with high speed GaAs chips provided as interfaces) enabling improved margins to be obtained by suppliers. Standardization in LANs (802.5, FDDI) will engender substantial growth and know-how transfer to installers will increase opportunities in private markets.

Gosling Associates' market research has suggested that standardization within test equipment will tend to reduce unit prices — at least in the short term. Single-mode fiber cable (described in Chapter 2) will be installed increasingly in new systems, ultimately including services directly to the business or domestic subscriber.

1

Introduction and overview

1.1 HISTORICAL SURVEY OF OPTICAL COMMUNICATIONS

Optical communications have really been with us longer than have electrical or radio communications — ever since creatures had eyes in fact. The development of optical instruments like telescopes and binoculars enabled people to view detail — shapes, signs and movements — out to the observable horizon in reasonable lighting and relatively clear weather.

Fire produces light and fire beacons, situated on prominent hilltops, have been used for communications over many thousands of years. Such beacon fires, on line-of-sight locations, brought Queen Clytemnestra news of the fall of Troy and of her husband's home-coming in 1184 BC.

A total distance of 900 km was covered in a series of relays — even today this would represent quite a significant line-of-sight terrestrial installation (see Fig. 1.1). Heliographs — reflecting sunlight under coded control — have been used in naval communications for a long time.

Modern communication systems, including fiber optics, are characterized by high speed, flexibility, reliability and international capability. People need to communicate directly (telephone, videophone), professional computer networks are extensively used, and sometimes TV must be communicated.

How in the area of optical communications has this capability evolved?

To obtain a historical perspective on light and optical communications consider the following developments.

Ancient Greece		Observation that light is guided by a piece of glass
1609	Galileo	Telescope
1873	Maxwell (UK)	Theoretical prediction of electromagnetic waves
1888	Hertz (Germany)	Confirmation of Maxwell's prediction, including the fact that light comprises such waves
1890	Tyndall (UK)	Observation that a thin water jet guides light
1930	Lamb (Germany)	Experiments with silica fiber
1951	Heel *et al* (UK)	Image transmission using optical bundles
1958	Goubau *et al* (US)	Lens guide
1958/59	Kapany *et al* (USA)	Clad optical fiber[*]
1960	Maiman *et al* (USA)	The ruby laser[*]
1962	Nathan *et al*; Holynak *et al*; etc (USA)	The semiconductor laser[*]
1966	Kao and Hockham (UK)	Optical fiber suggested for long-distance transmission
1969	Uchida *et al* and Kawakami and Nishizawa (Japan)	Special new design of fiber for low-delay transmission (called 'graded-index')[*]
1970	Kapron and Keck (USA)	Losses down to $20\,dB/km$[*]
1976	Rediffusion (London)	Fiber-optic cable connecting TV subscribers
1982	To present day: Main work in UK, some western European countries, USA and Japan	Losses down to $0.2\,dB/km$,[*] range over $100\,km$ commercial development

[*] Signifies a key development

Fig. 1.1 Fire-light communications of over 3000 years ago.

1.2 A SIMPLE LINK — MEDIUM COMPARISON

In the schematic diagram of a basic fiber-optic link a digital bit stream, obtained as data or from a telephone (as shown in Fig. 1.2), drives a semiconductor light source to produce light pulses.

At the receiver these impulses appear attenuated and widened due to the characteristics of the fiber. A photodiode converts the pulses back to electrical signals which can be amplified and regenerated to restore the original bit stream.

Relative to metal cables optical fibers have advantages in that they:

- have small diameters
- are lighter in weight and yet maintain flexibility and strength
- allow much greater distance to be covered without any amplifiers/ electronics
- give the possibility of extremely broad bandwidths
- naturally insulate between items of electrical equipment

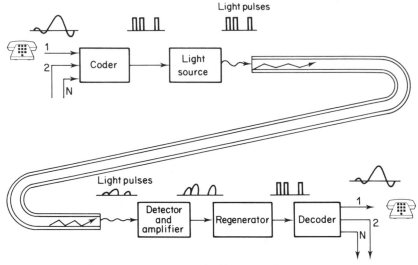

Fig. 1.2 How a simple fiber-optic link works.

- do not externally transmit any electromagnetic wave energy (it is extremely difficult to eavesdrop)
- are immune to interference due to other people's electrical equipment.

Against these advantages we must set the following drawbacks:

- each fiber has its own, restricting, bending radius. If bent more tightly than this the structure will lose a lot of its own light (mainly into buffer layers but some may radiate out) and will eventually break.
- connecting fibers together, and 'pigtailing' them to sources and detectors can present some difficulties for the designer — in particular, specialised equipment and skills are required — (most notable with single-mode fiber).
- some unit prices are relatively high — but are falling.
- unlike conducting wires electrical energy cannot be conveyed, even when desired.

The advantages are attractive and the drawbacks can be dealt with or tolerated, with appropriate systems design and installation.

In many situations, however, metallic cable communication media continue to provide the economic option. Examples include:

Table 1.1 Comparisons between some communication media

	Repeaters/ spacing	Broadcast/ point-to-point	Installation cost	Life* (years)	Weather effects — downtime	Operational radiation hazard	Eavesdropping (security problem)	Jamming	Mobile users
Broadcast radio and TV	Local re-broadcast	Broadcast	Moderate	Long	Yes, but minimal	Low-to-moderate	Yes	Yes	Yes
Ground-based line-of-sight microwave links	Frequent (line-of-sight)	Point-to-point	Moderate — depends on terrain	Long	Yes, but very small	High very close to transmitter	Yes	Yes	Yes
Communications satellites	One only (the satellite)	Broadcast ('spot' beams almost point-to-point)	High	Limited (10 years typical)	Yes, but very small	High close to transmitter	Yes	Yes	Yes
Tropospheric-scatter links	Few — 100 km or greater spacing	Point-to-point	Rather high	Long	Yes, downtime just significant	High	Yes	Yes	Semi-mobile
Coaxial (metallic) cables	Frequent — high losses	Point-to-point	Rather high	Long	No. Zero downtime	Very low	Yes	No	No
Optical fiber cables	Can be very few esp. single-mode	Point-to-point	Rather high†	Long	No. Zero downtime	Essentially zero	Very difficult	No	No

Notes: * 'Long' means typically several decades and assumes occasional replacement of electronics (except for satellites).
† Low if introduced into existing ducts, etc.

- subscriber's telephone line (especially domestic, and also often those within a large well-established business)
- internal electrical connections within a computer
- down-lead antenna to TV receiver: short distance, u.h.f.
- electrical links within local area networks (LANs — more about these later)
- waveguides for power microwave transmission (e.g. feeding a satellite communications transmitting antenna).

Several LANs already incorporate some optical fiber interconnections, and this is generally accepted as an expanding market for fiber optics.

Table 1.1 allows comparisons to be made between various communication media.

1.3 WHAT ARE FIBER-OPTIC SYSTEMS?

Because of its advantageous features (as described in the previous section), optical fiber technology is steadily increasing its penetration in a number of applications:

- closed-circuit television (CCTV)

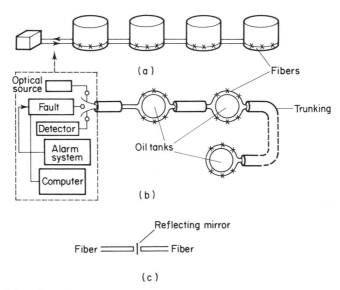

Fig. 1.3 Oil-tank movement sensing system (with grateful acknowledgment to Y. Suematsu and K.-I. Iga from whose work *Introduction to Optical Fiber Communications* this figure was taken with their permission).

- cable television (or 'community antenna' television) (CATV)
- local (or limited) area networks (LANs)
- metropolitan area networks (MANs)
- wide area networks (WANs)
- long-distance trunk communications
- non-communication applications such as instrumentation and sensors.

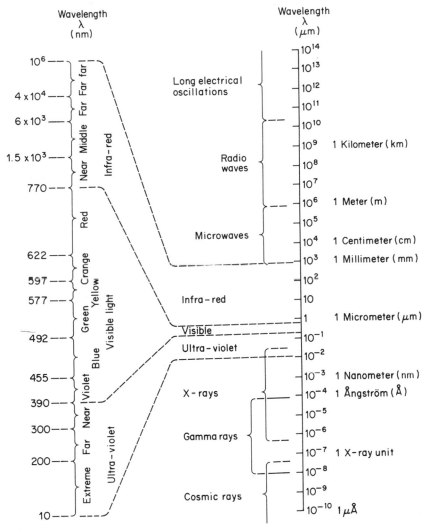

Fig. 1.4   The electromagnetic spectrum.

An oil tank installation movement sensing system is considered as a first practical example.

The use of electrical instruments or any circuitry in the vicinity of oil storage or fuel installations is essentially prohibited on the basis of intrinsic safety regulations.

The use of optical fibers eliminates this problem and an outline of a suitable fiber-optic system for sensing small movements is shown in Fig. 1.3.

At intervals around each tank (six are shown, in each case with an 'X') a simple mechanical mirror sensor normally transmits the light with only a relatively minor interruption. In the event of any tank movement the sensor shifts away, light transmission is severely interrupted, the detector output falls below a threshold and a computer-controlled alarm system is activated.

The location of the fault can be found by transmitting a pulse of light into one end of the fiber and measuring the delay time before the reflected pulse returns. Basically this is a simple form of optical time-domain reflectometry (OTDR) described in more detail in Chapter 8.

The electromagnetic spectrum (wavelengths) is shown in Fig. 1.4.

Fiber-optic systems generally operate at wavelengths in the near infra-red and the reasons for this are described in Chapter 2.

1.4 POWER BUDGET, ANALOG AND DIGITAL SIGNALS

1.4.1 Power budget

A simple and basic concept of power budget is shown in Fig. 1.5. Power budget diagrams are essential tools at the design stage and for link monitoring purposes. They enable the power levels to be determined at any location along a link — in general the link may use any communications technology: optical or otherwise.

Practical systems involve considerably more detail than shown here — in particular, cable discontinuities, connectors and splices are important. Detailed examples are considered later.

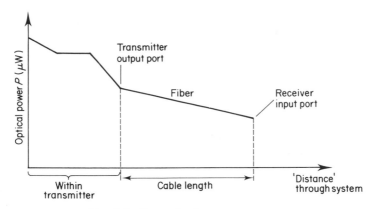

Fig. 1.5 Power budget concept.

1.4.2 *Modulation*

Amplitude Modulation (AM) is rarely used because of linearity problems but Frequency Modulation (FM) is sometimes used. The waveform of the optical power then appears as shown in Fig. 1.6.

Modulation for digital transmission is, in current fiber-optic systems, performed by rapidly (almost always electronically) turning the light *on* and *off* or between two distinct levels, according to the requirements (1 or 0) of the bit streams. For a byte comprising 01010011 the optical power waveform might appear as shown in Fig. 1.7.

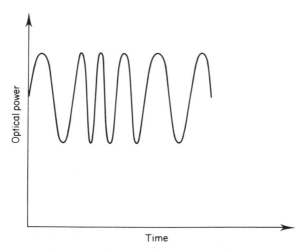

Fig. 1.6 FM optical power waveform.

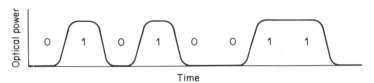

Fig. 1.7 One possible waveform for a digital signal.

This process is generally termed an amplitude-shift-keying (ASK) or 'on-off-keying' (OOK) modulation scheme. The power levels are not necessarily fully *on* for a 1 and fully *off* for a 0.

This means that all installed/commercially available fiber-optic systems of the late 1980s and early 1990s are strictly *baseband*.

1.4.3 Bit error rate (BER)

(Also sometimes known as the probability of bit error.) This is the

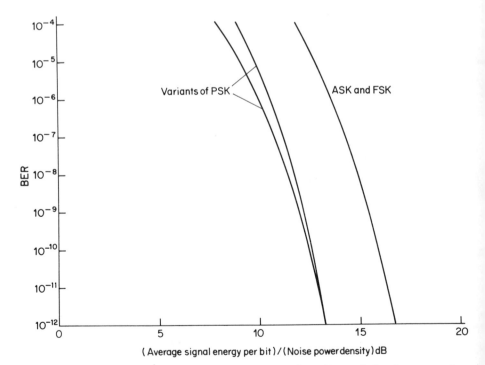

Fig. 1.8 BER versus received signal-to-noise power for ASK, and also for some other types of modulation.

probability of the receiver actually reproducing a bit of the transmitted information erroneously, i.e. a 1 for a 0 or vice versa.

The tolerable maximum values of BER depend upon the service for which the system is designed.

Fundamentally, BER is a function of:

- received signal-to-noise (S/N) ratio
- modulation scheme.

The higher the received S/N ratio, the lower (better) will be the BER.

- for speech channels around 10^{-3} is tolerable
- digital TV requires considerably better than this $(10^{-5}, 10^{-6})$
- data transmission demands generally BER below 10^{-8}
- LANs and MANs require: 10^{-5} to 10^{-12}.

The majority of LANs specify 'better than 10^{-9}'.

For these baseband-modulated optical systems BER varies smoothly with received 'signal-to-noise' power ratio as shown in Fig. 1.8.

2

Fibers and fiber cables

2.1 MULTIMODE AND SINGLE-MODE FIBERS

In this chapter optical fibers, their characteristics and limitations, and cable assemblies incorporating the fibers are considered. Most (but not all) of the fibers are made of silica.

The two main classes of fiber are:

● multimode
● single-mode (or 'monomode').

Multimode further subdivides into:

● multimode step-index
● multimode graded-index.

Multimode fibers are generally used at modest information rates — most often up to some tens of Mbits/s — and for ranges up to 10 km or so. Although over 300 Mbit/s has been sent over an 8 km multimode fiber, a more usual situation would be (say) 140 Mbit/s pulse-code modulated (PCM) carrying 1400 telephone channels over 7 km between repeaters. More frequently these types of fibers carry computer network data at rates varying from some Kbit/s to over 100 Mbit/s.

Multimode fibers are also extensively used in optical-fiber-based LANs.

Single-mode fibers are finding application mainly in medium- to long-distance trunk communications systems and international systems (e.g. 565 Mbit/s). There is a trend for these fibers to penetrate increasingly into market sectors previously occupied by multimode due to falling prices and increasing bit-rate requirements.

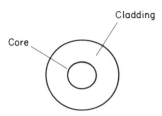

Fig. 2.1   The basic transverse cross-section through a step-index fiber.

Currently single-mode fibers cost approximately the same per unit length as multimode fibers of reasonably high quality.

A very basic transverse cross-section through a step-index fiber is shown in Fig. 2.1.

Multimode fibers have a multitude of rays ('modes') travelling within them. Some of the rays travel more slowly than others because they take significantly different overall routes. For instance, some rays will hardly change direction at all, whereas others will zigzag greatly in any given length of fiber.

Whether a fiber will support one or more modes (i.e. will be single-mode or multimode) depends critically on the core diameter relative to the light wavelength.

Provided the core is no more than a few wavelengths in diameter, i.e. a few microns in practice, only one mode is propagated and we have single-mode fiber.

The step-index cross-section structure is the simplest to consider. There is a multimode example of step index and single-mode is inherently step index.

Some typical fiber-interior transverse cross-sections are shown in Fig. 2.2.

Notice that the largest dimension in any of these structures is one-eighth of a millimeter — which is one-to-two orders of magnitude smaller than typical metallic (electrical) coaxial cable dimensions. When the fiber is incorporated within a simple cable, however, the overall diameter is of the same order as that of coaxial cable.

The step-index fiber structure results in considerable time delays in the arrival of the rays at the receiver. This causes the bandwidth to be restricted to about 25 or 30 MHz over a few km link. Higher bandwidths over longer links can be obtained by using a rather more expensive fiber, the refractive index of which is graded from core to cladding. These 'graded index' fibers can cover link routes up to about 10 km at moderate bandwidths or data rates.

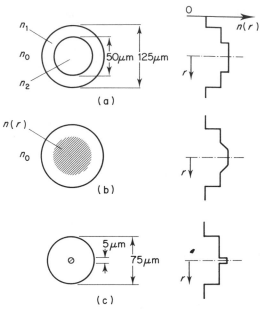

Fig. 2.2 Transverse cross-sections through several representative types of fibers. (a) Multimode step-index fiber (typical dimensions), (b) parabolically graded index fiber (multimode), (c) monomode or single-mode step-index fiber (typical dimensions).

All-plastic ('polymer') fibers

These are quite adequate for transferring signals at relatively slow information rates over fairly short distances where the environment is reasonably benign. This may seem very restrictive but such polymer fibers are finding increasing applications. As the distance approaches one kilometer these fibers become less practical owing to the large loss of power — hundreds of dB per km at this writing.

These plastic fibers may be appropriate for highly localized application (e.g. automobile data buses, VLANs).

Acceptance angle and numerical aperture (NA)

A maximum angle, called the acceptance angle θc, exists above which light projected into a fiber end (from a LED or a laser) will not be propagated along the fiber.

To avoid misunderstanding over units (degrees, radians, etc), the sine of half this acceptance angle, called the numerical aperture (NA), is often used to specify fibers and fiber-based systems.

$$NA = \sin (\theta c/2)$$

The plastic fibers just described have numerical apertures between 0.5 and 0.6 — light within a cone of about $60°$ will actually enter the fiber when NA = 0.5.

Many glass step-index fibers have an NA of only about 0.2, implying only a $23°$ cone of 'allowable' light. About 70% of the total available light from a laser would enter but only about 15% of light from a surface-emitting LED would enter such a fiber (unless lensed, see Chapter 4).

Single-mode fibers

To ensure the existence of only one mode the diameter of the core must be made, at most, only a few wavelengths of light. This means that core diameters are an order of magnitude smaller than those given for the previous structures, being typically of the order of a few micrometers. A direct result of the single mode is that only one speed and one trajectory apply and thus delays are almost zero.

Thus, cables with single-mode fibers can be used for

- long-distance transmission (trunk telecomms), and/or

- very high data rates (hundreds/thousands of Mbit/s).

Applications include national and international trunk networks, and special circumstances (e.g. radar distribution, extremely high bit-rate links).

There is a trend towards increased use of single-mode fibers in many applications. Apart from their great bandwidths these single-mode fibers, with their near-zero delays and extremely small energy losses, can currently span long distances; up towards 100 km without interruptions at, say, 140 Mbit/s.

Several companies manufacture and supply single-mode fibers, for example: Corning-Glass (USA), Optical Fibers (UK) and CLTO (France).

2.2 POWER LOSSES (FIBER ATTENUATION)

Attenuation, or transmission loss, is a significant feature of any optical fiber. This varies greatly from one type of fiber to another and it is always dependent upon wavelength.

Recent improvements in fiber fabrication have resulted in reducing the impurity content in the fiber to around 50 parts per billion. The loss minimum in these newer products occurs at a longer wavelength (>1200 nm) than that for the earlier fibers and losses of less than 0.15 dB/km have been achieved in single-mode.

The important point about these newer fibers is that both minimum attenuation and minimum total dispersion occur around 1200–1300 nm and again at 1550 nm and this has led to a need for lasers, LEDs and photodiodes capable of efficient operation at these wavelengths.

The detailed loss versus wavelength curves are important and typical results are shown in Fig. 2.3.

A number of mechanisms are responsible for these losses: particularly scattering ('Rayleigh') and molecular resonance absorption. We shall not enter into further details here.

The most commonly encountered fiber type, the commercial multimode, shows loss minima typically at about 800–830 nm, 980 nm and 1100 nm. Operation at these wavelengths is best — where possible.

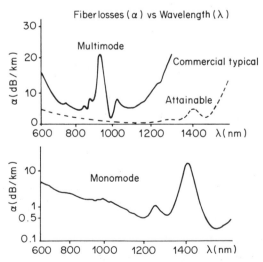

Fig. 2.3 Typical fiber losses (attenuation) as a function of wavelength.

Study of the single-mode curve reveals two further 'windows', at 1300 nm and 1550 nm. An extremely low loss of 0.15 dB/km is available at 1550 nm. This means that 15 dB would be lost in a 100 km continuous length of such fiber — one hundredth of the input power would emerge at the receiver (e.g. 1 mW input into the fiber, 10 μW output).

Temperature and humidity effects

With temperatures cycled from 125 °C to 200 °C over 14 days, or 98% humidity cycling, multimode fibers exhibit less than 0.3 dB/km change and single-mode less than 0.1 dB/km change. In both cases the variations are less than 0.2 dB/km with the temperature at − 60 °C.

Nuclear radiation effects

Choice of core material strongly influences the ability to recover from gamma-radiation dosage, and under extremely high radiation doses irreversible core damage can occur. Applications where this is important include:

- nuclear reactor installations
- high-energy laboratories
- military (chiefly tactical).

Exposure to gamma-radiation increases the optical loss in all fibers and the greater the length of fiber exposed to the radiation the more the additional loss. Also, for radiation doses below 2000 rad, the extra loss depends on the amount of radiation received. It is also generally true that fibers with low inherent losses (i.e. those starting with low loss) exhibit relatively small radiation-induced loss. Most defense applications call for step-index fibers since very often a bandwidth × length product of only a few MHz km is required. Thus fairly inexpensive step-index plastic-clad-silica (PCS) fibers are useful in this respect. It has been observed that the selection of PCS fibers with an appreciable water content, given a very large radiation dose and then allowed to anneal, become effectively 'hardened' against subsequent radiation effects (this advantage is most marked at 850 nm, less pronounced at 1300 nm).

Table 2.1 $B \times L$ product comparisons for various transmission media

Transmission medium	Typical $B \times L$ product (MHz $\times$ km)
Twisted wire pair	1
Coaxial cable	20
Optical fiber	400 (and up)

Since both dispersion and attenuation are length-dependent we can very usefully characterize fiber by bandwidth $\times$ length ($B \times L$). The units are most often MHx $\times$ km, but can be as high as GHz $\times$ km. Optical fiber can be compared with other commonly used transmission media, in $B \times L$ terms and the general results are shown in Table 2.1. The relatively high value of $B \times L$ available with fiber represents a *fundamental advantage for this transmission medium.*

This advantage is mainly a consequence of the low dispersion that can be obtained, since the bandwidth of optical fibers is ultimately dispersion limited.

Comparison with metal cable

Metallic cables (coaxial and twisted wire), in contrast to fiber, have their bandwidth's attenuation limited. Electrical loss mechanisms (particularly the one called the 'skin effect') cause restrictions at considerably lower frequencies. There are irreducible limits to these losses — no special design approaches such as 'graded-index' or 'dispersion'-shifting are available with metallic cables.

2.3 DISPERSION AND BANDWIDTH

At moderate-to-high bit rates and/or medium-to-long distance dispersion dictates the feasible limits for (bandwidth) $\times$ (distance) products.

There are three mechanisms in fibers that can cause this unwanted dispersion:

- modal
- material (or 'chromatic')
- waveguide.

The first mechanism, modal dispersion, only occurs in multimode fibers and is minimized by using graded-index. It is manifested as different transit or 'journey' times associated with different ray or 'mode' paths.

The second, material or 'chromatic' dispersion, can occur in any fiber — including single mode. It is due to the variation of refractive index with wavelength and the spectral linewidth of the transmitter source therefore becomes important here. Again, variable delays occur.

Therefore, to reduce the effect of dispersion, it is better to use a laser (with the inherent relatively narrow linewidth) than an LED for transmission. More details are given in Chapter 4.

Waveguide dispersion occurs in single-mode fibers but, by selecting an operating wavelength appropriately, the material dispersion can be arranged to cancel this ('dispersion-shifting' — an important relatively new technique). Philips NV of Eindhoven (Netherlands) is now producing dispersion-flattened single-mode fiber which can carry two optical wavelengths simultaneously — with low loss and near-zero dispersion. With this fiber dispersion is under 3.5 ps/nm-km at both 1310 nm and 1550 nm — and the attenuation does not exceed 0.5 dB/km and 0.3 dB/km at each respective wavelength. Corning Glass offer dispersion-shifted single-mode fibers (dispersion minimum shifted to 1550 nm, rather than the more usual 1300 nm), while retaining the low loss of 0.21 dB/km at this wavelength.

The main overall effect of all dispersion, on digital signals, is the spreading of pulses of light as they travel down the fiber and this is shown in Fig. 2.4.

At the receiver, the spread output pulse will eventually be read as two 1s instead of the original single 1. This means increased bit errors, i.e. a higher bit error rate (BER). This problem worsens with increasing bit rate and/or range.

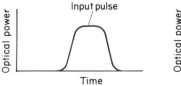 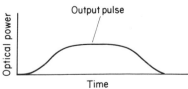

Fig. 2.4 Input and output pulses for a digital optical fiber system, indicating the principal effect of dispersion.

2.4 FIBER MANUFACTURING

Multicomponent glasses are made from traditional optical glass-forming constituents such as borosilicate glass and have the advantage of relatively low melting-points so that conventional melting techniques can be employed, including radio-frequency crucible and resistance-heated muffle furnaces.

Most fiber manufacturers use variants on the chemical-vapor deposition (CVD) technique. The chief requirements of this technique are indicated in Fig. 2.5.

The basic CVD process was developed by Corning in the USA; it is still used by this company and is licenced to many European manufacturers (e.g. FOS in Italy, FOI and Cables de Lyon in France). Deposition of both core and cladding makes possible wide variation and precise tailoring of the refractive index profile so that multimode, single-mode and large-core high-NA fibers can be produced.

The MCVD (modified chemical vapor deposition) method was developed at Bell Laboratories and is also widely used in the US, Europe and Japan. Here the core material is deposited within a silica tube which forms the cladding part of the preform. A modification of this process known as PMCVD (plasma modified chemical vapor deposition) has been developed by Bell to obtain higher deposition rates and efficiencies. In addition to the normal MCVD techniques an RF coil around the tube generates an internal high temperature plasma. It is

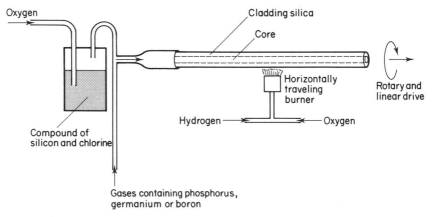

Fig. 2.5 Principle of the chemical vapor deposition (CVD) method of optical fiber manufacture.

particularly well-suited to fabrication of single-mode and large-core high-NA fibers.

Philips in the Netherlands have also developed and use in production a plasma-based method (PCVD).

Material costs are steadily becoming a more significant component of final price as fabrication costs fall.

Dimensions

The most important dimension is the core diameter (this dictates, in part, compatible sources, etc). Next we have the cladding diameter and finally it is important to note typical outer diameters (OD). Most manufacturers give core and cladding diameters, many in the form:

'x/y fiber'
e.g. 62.5/125 fiber

which means a 62.5 μm diameter core and 125 μm diameter cladding.

Some typical, practically *de facto*, standards are indicated in Table 2.2.

Bending fibers will eventually induce extra losses. In the long term (permanent installation) stresses caused by bending may result in fiber failure due to internal fracture.

Tensile strength

The tensile strength of optical fiber cables is substantially greater than that of copper cables having similar diameter. Maximum figures quoted by manufacturers vary from 4 kg to 300 N force load (suppliers are not consistent in their use of units for such 'forces').

Table 2.2 Dimensions of some optical fibers

Fiber type	$x/y(\mu m)$
Step or graded index	62.5/125, 50/125 or 100/140
Step-index; silica core	200/300 (very occasionally).

Hydrogen effect (longer wavelengths)

Attenuation increases can occur, at 1300 nm and above, particularly if fiber is germanium doped. Some cables can generate hydrogen in the presence of water.

Therefore choice of cable materials is vital and sealing against water ingress is important.

2.5 FIBER CABLE STRUCTURES

The simple, basic, fiber structure of core and cladding glasses (or plastics) is inadequate on its own. It must in practice be surrounded by several extra layers of materials and a typical construction for a simple cable is shown in Fig. 2.6.

The silicone coating and buffer jacket protect the fiber from moisture and abrasion, as well as preventing the escape of light.

Bending radii. This depends on whether short-term or permanent installation radii are considered. Reasonable rules-of-thumb are, for minimum radii:

Short term: 3 × OD   ⎧ for cables
                                 ⎨ at least a
Permanently   10 × OD   ⎩ few mm OD
installed:

For many data communication applications cable assemblies comprising 2 to 10 internal fibers are available. Polymer spacing, reinforcing and flexural tubes are incorporated to make up the complete cables and handling and installation may be similar to that for conventional metallic cables — in some cases easier. 'Hybrid' cables, containing a mixture of fiber optic and metallic, are also available. The numerical apertures (NA) of fibers within such fiber cables are typically 0.25 and losses can be as high as 10 dB/km. Large numbers of optical fibers, up to 2000 or so, may be combined into a more complex overall cable structure supplied by companies such as Siemens (telecomms). A modest example containing only four fibers is shown in Fig. 2.7.

Two points should be noted regarding multi-fiber cables:

● crosstalk between fibers is virtually zero and (in theory at least) they can be closely packed;

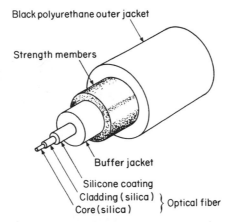

Fig. 2.6 A simple optical fiber cable suitable for relatively benign indoor environments: outside diameter typically about 5 mm. (Taken from commercial product application information available from the Hewlett-Packard Company.)

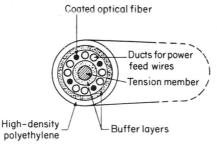

Fig. 2.7 An example of a reinforced cable structure (with grateful acknowledgment to Y. Suematsu and K.-I. Iga from whose work *Introduction to Optical Fiber Communications* this figure was taken with their permission).

- electrical power lines may be combined within the same unit (e.g. to supply repeaters).

The structure shown in Figs. 2.6 and 2.7 would be suitable for relatively benign land-based (predominantly indoor) environments. For larger assemblies several clusters of main internal units are typical, each containing subsidiary units themselves comprising five to ten fiber clusters.

High-tensile armouring, with internal support members and cushioning, are used within such units. The final assembly usually has its interstices filled with a polymer-based compound, to maintain flexibility.

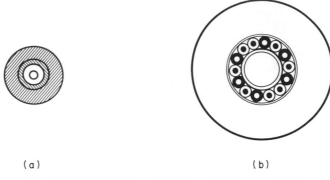

(a)   (b)

Fig. 2.8   Tight buffer cable (a) and final assembly (b).

We next consider a number of other significant cable structures, staring with tight buffer cable.

In tight buffer designs (Fig. 2.8) the fiber is protected by extrusions of synthetic compounds such as silicone leading to an overall diameter of about 1 mm. The final coating beyond the silicone is usually nylon. These types of cables are worthy of consideration in situations where significant *strain* is anticipated.

For *high-count cables*, typically containing 30 or more fibers, loose tube implementation tends to predominate. In these structures the fibers are set, loosely, within polymer tubes and under such conditions the fibers themselves are rarely, if ever, subject to strain.

Cables suited to the local loop

Many local loop (subscriber, LAN, MAN, etc) demands and conditions differ considerably from those of the trunk network. In particular, suitable cables must meet the following requirements:

- fiber mechanical protection (as in the trunk network)
- protection/precautions against optical degradation (low power devices used — reduced link margin)
- splice-intensive network — cable must accommodate
- cable design must be cost-effective
- occasionally, power feed may be required
- high fiber counts are involved (loose tube designs)
- installation conditions relatively hazardous.

An example of multiple fibers set loosely in tubes is shown in Fig. 2.9.

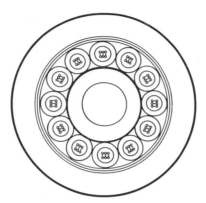

Fig. 2.9 One possible type of cable structure that may be suitable for local loop (subscriber connection) applications.

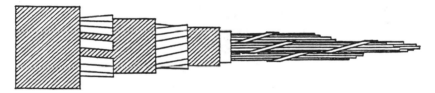

Fig. 2.10 The ATT 'Lightpack' cable structure.

Problems with this include:

● not easy to splice (especially when fully filled)
● almost certainly not cheapest type of product.

Another possibility is the *ATT 'Lightpack'*, the longitudinal cross-section of which is shown in Fig. 2.10.

The simplicity of the cable interior whereby the fibers are bundled with yarn into simple units is achieved through having a very high strength sheath incorporating two layers of steel wire armouring applied helically. Consequently the main advantage is ease of manufacture and the chief disadvantage is unsuitability for use with very high fiber counts.

Ribbon-based cables

These were pioneered by ATT in the early 1970s and they have been extensively used by that company.

Currently several companies have developed various versions of these types of cables (particularly in the UK and in Japan).

Attractions of the technology include:

- simple, inexpensive manufacture
- permits in-process splicing
- good choice for long cables (local loop)
- facilitates possible mass splicing.

One problem imposed by the ribbon approach is that flat arrays do not pack well into cylindrical cables. Various designs are available and transverse cross-sections of some are shown in Figs. 2.11 through 2.14.

Fig. 2.11 Ribbon stack cable structure (due originally to ATT).

Fig. 2.12 Ribbon-in-tube cable structure (due originally to Furukawa).

Fig. 2.13 Slotted core cable structure (promoted by several companies).

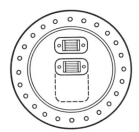

Fig. 2.14 A fiber cable structure based upon ribbon stacks oriented in flat tubes.

There are conflicting requirements in all these examples. For manu-facturing and splicing productivity wide ribbons with 10 to 12 fibers are desirable. On the other hand for high cable packing densities narrow ribbons are best.

A compromise design is therefore required. One possibility is the use of ribbon stacks housed in flat tubes undulated in cable (this also provides a margin against strain). Such a structure is indicated in Fig. 2.14. This structure, which it is believed was first suggested by Taylor of BICC, is claimed to be relatively easy to manufacture, easy to splice and avoids stranding.

2.6 INSTALLATION CONSIDERATIONS

It is generally recommended that cables be installed in sections for easy maintenance and to readily allow for future expansion. This approach is indicated in Fig. 2.15.

Other important installation aspects are now discussed under the headings 'indoor' and 'outdoor' — Figs. 2.16 and 2.17.

Indoor

Under carpets or matting. Install below a pad for better protection of carpeting; beware of heavy, sharp traffic or loads. (Applies to all cables.) *Taped along baseboards.* Beware of corners — observe the minimum bend radius (very important with fibers). *Through rubber*

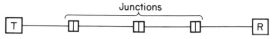

Fig. 2.15 Section-by-section cable installation.

floor duct. Employ double mitering at corners to enlarge the bend radius in the duct.

It is generally recommended that a maximum of ten, 3 mm cables be installed in a ½-inch diameter duct — up to a maximum of 29 such cables in a 1-inch duct.

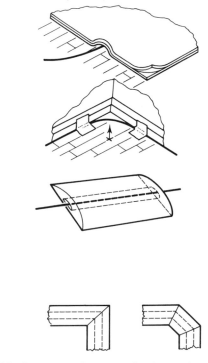

Fig. 2.16   Important features of indoor cable installation.

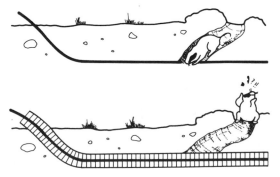

Fig. 2.17   Important features of outdoor cable installation.

Outdoor

Direct burial. Cable design must withstand abuse during installation and underground hazards such as ingress of moisture (e.g. hydrogen effects). Rodent attack must also be guarded against.

Indirect burial. Cable may be pulled into pre-buried duct or pre-installed in flexible 'leaktight' tubes.

Advantages. Thermal stability (install below frostline) and protection from surface hazards (chiefly traffic).

Cable cost comparisons

A useful measure of cost efficiency is offered by the following ratio:

$$\left(\frac{\text{COST}}{B \times L}\right) = \left(\frac{\$}{\text{MHz} \times \text{km}}\right)$$

At current prices appropriate comparative data are given in Table 2.3.

Table 2.3 Media pricing comparisons

Transmission medium	$(\text{Cost}/B \times L)$ $(\$/\text{MHz} \times \text{km})$
Twisted wire pair	15
Coaxial cable	18
Optical fiber	1

These figures are based upon twisted wire pair at 1.5 cents/m, 'coax' at 15 cents/m and optical fiber cable at about 30 cents/m.

Cable assemblies involve increased costs in all cases (metallic and optical fiber).

Two significant points are:

- 'Short' (tens of metres) cables tend to be dominated by connector costs
- Installation costs and repeater amplifier costs have not been considered. Installation costs usually exceed, by far, the cable cost.

SUMMARY TABLE

Table 2.4 Optical fibers summary

	Classes and types of fiber		
	Multimode		Single-mode
	Plastic	Glass	
Typical core diameter (mm)	1.0	0.0625	0.005 -
Maximum achievable bandwidth	A few MHz	Around 1 GHz	Several GHz (now) 25 000 GHz (future)
Usual operating bandwidth	Several kHz	Several MHz	Hundreds of MHz
Approximate maximum link distances	100 m	30 km	200 km
Approximate cost ($ per meter)	0.1 (system also cheap)	0.1	0.1*

* System more expensive owing to greater cost of couplers, sources, detectors etc.

3

Connectors, couplers, splicers and 'WDM'

3.1 CONNECTORS

There exists a wide choice of components available for interconnecting any type of cable (electrical or otherwise) and yet the ultimate decision can often be critical. Often the choice of connector is the most important decision to be made.

A number of *de facto* standards now exist for optical fiber cable connectors depending on requirement and application. A representative list is given:

- 'quick' terminations (e.g. Leetec's 'Rapid Termination')
- improved quality: FMA style
- high quality: PC/FC
- special applications: Biconic, or ST
- military connectors (e.g. MIL-C-38999)
- multiple-fiber connectors
- single-mode connectors.

Major goals of connector design include:

- low coupling losses following many demountings and remountings (disconnections and reconnections)
- interchangeability with similar type connectors
- low sensitivity to environment conditions (e.g. temperature, moisture and dust)
- ease of connection
- reliability of connection (ruggedness)
- simple and inexpensive manufacture.

FMA-style connectors are the 'optical equivalent' of the SMA miniature coaxial threaded electrical versions which are used for well-shielded high-frequency applications. These FMA connectors are relatively inexpensive but tend to be subject to moderate loss and poor repeatability performance.

PC or FC connectors are of the ferrule type — occasionally referred to as the concentric sleeve design. The accurate alignment sleeve within this (Fig. 3.1) ensures relatively low losses and good repeatability.

For further performance improvements a watch-jewel alignment section is incorporated into such FC connectors.

In other applications biconic connectors incorporating tapered plastic moulding aligners, or the newer 'ST' designs are available. Biconic designs are often favoured in telecommunications applications. ST connectors are strictly straight ferrule designs but they incorporate:

● bayonet coupling (i.e. in similar style to BNC electrical connectors)
● ceramic capillaries
● split alignment sleeves.

Typical manufacturers are AT & T and AMP, and it is thought that ST connectors will find increasing application in limited area data networks.

AT & T and AMP have also recently been very active in duplex connector design for the FDDI (see Chapter 6) 100 Mbit/s local network standard.

For single-channel applications, the military have favoured the SMA-style connector (EIA standard, also MIL-C-83522; adopted by NATO). Where multichannel applications are concerned the MIL-C-38999 is standard (Fig. 3.2) and ITT-Cannon typify manufacturers of such connectors.

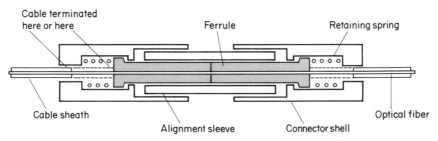

Fig. 3.1 Longitudinal cross-section of the basic ferrule connector (FC) (with grateful acknowledgment to John Senior from whose work *Optical Fiber Communications*, published by Prentice-Hall in 1985, this figure was taken with permission).

Fig. 3.2 An example of MIL-C-38999 (military) connectors (with grateful acknowledgment to ITT-Cannon who are thanked for providing this photograph).

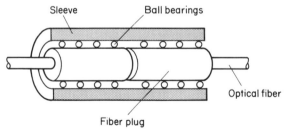

Fig. 3.3 Longitudinal cross-section of the basic single-mode fiber connector (with
grateful acknowledgment to John Senior from whose work *Optical Fiber
Communications*, published by Prentice-Hall in 1985, this figure was taken with
permission).

Multiple-fiber connectors (apart from the military version just
described) are sometimes formed in ribbon cable structures — with
elaborate V-grooved silicon and sprung alignment systems.

Single-mode connectors usually employ a sleeve, plug and ball-
bearing alignment arrangement as indicated in Fig. 3.3.

In trunk telecommunications systems, which are the main application for single-mode fiber optics, cables are spliced throughout. As single-mode technology penetrates ever closer to the end user however the availability of suitable connectors will become increasingly important. It is not certain that sleeved ball-bearing arrangements will meet the demand here.

3.2 OPTICAL COUPLERS

Couplers are required in many systems, including 'local' or limited area networks (LANs) based on fiber optics and they can also be used in some test and measurement situations. A common arrangement comprises a directional coupler made from two fused fibers, called a twisted-pair coupler (see Fig. 3.4).

It is customary to use the term 'ports' for the connection 'points': 1, 2, 1′, 2′. This configuration can also be considered as a T-coupler in the more restrictive case where only three ports are used. The twisted pair is manufactured by twisting the fibers, then pulling them into biconical tapers under heat treatment.

In the fused section the fiber cores are still physically separated from each other but 'core modes' are converted to 'cladding modes', thus partly coupling optical power from one fiber to the other. A unit such as this providing a 50% output power split is called a 3 dB coupler. As this is a directional coupler (also called a transmissive coupler), there is some degree of isolation between the two input ports.

A number of other T-coupler technologies have also been realized. One approach comprises a joint of one input fiber with two side-by-side output fibers, another alternative amounts to imaging an input fiber onto two output fibers via concave mirrors. Also possible is a plain half-transparent mirror oriented at a 45° angle in conjunction with beam collimation. There are also transmissive and reflective star couplers (see Fig. 3.5).

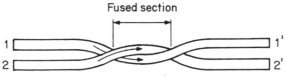

Fig. 3.4 The fused-section twisted-pair fiber coupler.

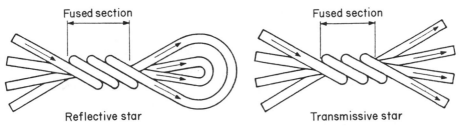

Fig. 3.5 Transmissive and reflective star couplers.

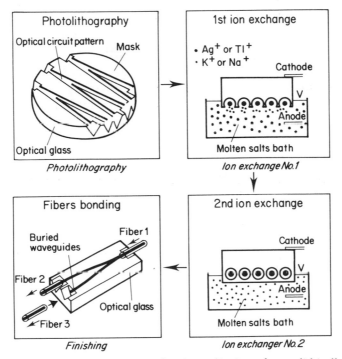

Fig. 3.6 Manufacturing process steps for the realisation of monolithically integrated optical components (with grateful acknowledgment to Corning-France from whose published product information this figure was taken with permission).

These types of couplers have been used in some types of data networks (e.g. 'star-LANs').

It is also possible and advantageous to consider planar monolithic approaches. Corning-France (a subsidiary of Corning Glass) introduced their 'Photocor' integrated optical couplers to the market in April 1987. The products embody a new approach and technology — briefly summarized in Fig. 3.6.

The typical finally assembled product is about 10 cm long and 1 cm square cross-section.

Loss (attenuation) and power-splitting mechanisms are broadly indicated in Fig. 3.7. The optical attenuation from an input to an output port in this type of coupler depends upon four factors:

A1 : linear attenuation within the coupler.
A2, A3 : attenuation at the fiber–coupler interface.
A4 : power splitting.

Accurate (and highly repeatable) control of the integrated manufacturing process determines the important splitting ratio (A4): nominally 3 dB for a 1:2 coupler, nominally 6 dB for a 1:4, etc. Linear and fiber-coupler interface attenuations are minimized by careful design and technology — again having advantages through this integrated circuit

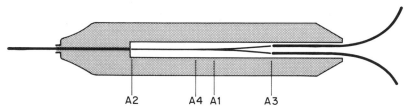

Fig. 3.7 Schematic diagram of an integrated optical coupler (with grateful acknowledgement to Corning-France from whose published product information this figure was taken with permission)

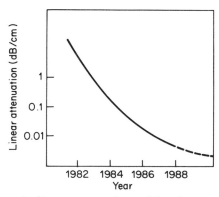

Fig. 3.8 Improvements in linear attenuation achieved over development years for integrated optical couplers (with grateful acknowledgment to Corning-France from whose published product information this figure was taken with permission).

approach. Improvements obtained in linear attenuation, 1982 to current, are shown in Fig. 3.8.

Applications are in star (and other) data networks — and in fiber-optic sensor systems.

The current 'Photocor' multimode products will be followed by single-mode products.

Any coupler is chiefly characterized by the quantities:

- insertion loss
- coupling ratio
- excess loss, and
- isolation.

Definitions are:

$$\text{Insertion loss} = \frac{\text{optical power from any single output}}{\text{optical power input}}$$

$$\text{Coupling ratio} = \frac{\text{optical power from any single output}}{\text{total optical power output}}$$

$$\text{Excess loss} = \frac{\text{total optical power output}}{\text{optical power input}}$$

(taking '10 log' in each case gives dB).

The isolation is a measure of the unwanted degree of 'crosstalk' between outputs. Some typical specification data for a 1:8 coupler integrated coupler (Corning) is:

- Insertion loss   10.5 dB
- Excess loss   1.5 dB
- Isolation   40.0 dB
- Uniformity of these data (maximum excursion): 1.5 dB.

This specification holds over the wavelength range 600–1600 nm and the temperature range -25 to $+70$ °C.

Other 'figures of merit' include uniformity of coupling ratio with changing wavelength (and from one fiber to another) and lack of dependence on fiber modes.

There are two further quantities that are often referred to in connection with couplers: directivity and return loss. (These quantities are also familiar where electrical signal couplers are under consideration.)

Directivity is a measure of the undesired fraction of power coupled back into an adjacent port and return loss is a measure of the (again undesired) power reflected back from the input port. Both quantities would normally be expected to be 'low' — typically 30 dB or 40 dB down on the input power level.

It must be appreciated that after coupling ratio and excess loss have been accounted for, connector losses at all ports of the coupler must be added.

3.3   FIBER SPLICING

The need to maximize repeater spacings on fiber-optic cables in long-haul networks requires connections to be minimum-loss. This is particularly important with single-mode fiber since a loss of 0.3 dB represents approximately 1 km of fiber attenuation. Thus the preferred connection is a low-loss splice when there is no requirement for it to be demountable.

Fusion is the most frequently used field technique for low-loss splicing and special-purpose electric-arc fusion-splicers are readily available (manufactured by companies such as STC, BICC, Siemens) which can weld high melting-point silica glasses. These splicers are fitted with microscope viewers and precise fiber positioning and clamping arrangements. Gas-flame fusion-splicers are also available and experimental work has been carried out in Japan on fusion with a CO_2 laser. These units frequently incorporate arrangements to give an automatic sequence of pre-fusion, fiber-end feeding and final fusion once manual positioning is completed. Tolerances for single-mode fiber are high and it is essential to maintain accurate core-alignment at the 1 micron level or less and for end-faces to be cut accurately. This level of alignment accuracy is achieved by using active piezoelectric transducers which shift the fiber radially until maximum light transmission is achieved. At this time the fibers are automatically fused.

After splicing the fibers are protected by, for example, a metal splice-connector crimped to the cable outer and subsequently covered with air-curing silicone rubber. The whole assembly is then supported and protected by a container or closure to avoid damage and provide effective mechanical cable continuity. Around six spliced terminations can be produced per hour by a semi-skilled technician using these techniques.

Splices are also occasionally required in more accessible situations, such as local data links and networks, often using multimode fiber cables. Occasionally some form of fusion splicer can be used in such situations and the present trend is towards increased use of such equipment.

Currently, low-cost techniques such as axial pin alignment assemblies and heat-shrinkable plastic overlays are often used.

3.4 WAVELENGTH-DIVISION MULTIPLEXERS (WDM)

The telecommunications industry is well used, electrically, to a technique known as frequency-division-multiplexing (FDM) in which channels for information transfer are separated in identified and usually equal frequency bands. WDM is, to a first rough approximation, the optical equivalent of FDM.

Several companies offer devices which separate and redirect optical signals at two or more wavelengths: duplexers and WDM devices (manufacturers include Siemens, Optometrics, Telefunken, Sumitomo, Amphenol). A number of approaches exist to the realization of such components.

One technology for forming an optical duplexer is indicated in Fig. 3.9 together with a ray path schematic of the component (many companies use these in trade or application literature).

The hemispherical ends of the transmission and receiver fibers, formed by fusion in an electric arc, act as lenses and thus reduce the coupling losses caused by expansion of the beam between the fibers. The wavelengths are isolated by a dielectric multilayer interference filter on the oblique ground end of the transmitter fiber.

The filter is designed so that it fully transmits the light from the transmitter and reflects the light to the receiver. Filtering layers can be evaporated onto a large number of suitably prepared fiber ends simultaneously, thus permitting cost-efficient manufacture.

Transmission losses at each wavelength (850 and 1300 nm) are below 1.5 dB and crosstalk (isolation) is less than 30 dB.

Hybrid integrated duplexers have also been developed in which all the components (including optoelectronic) are combined in one module.

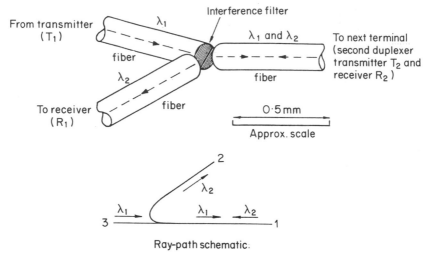

Ray-path schematic.

Fig. 3.9 A two-wavelength optical duplexer (with grateful acknowledgment to AEG of West Germany from whose published product information this figure was taken with permission).

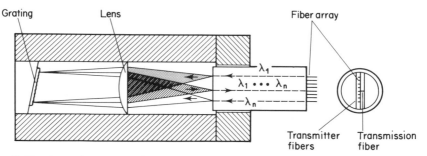

Fig. 3.10 A grating-type multiplexer (with grateful acknowledgment to AEG of West Germany from whose published product information this figure was taken with permission).

WDM components can be formed using grating multiplexer principles and such a component (cross-sections) is shown in Fig. 3.10.

In these multiplexers a single fiber (the transmission fiber) is fed with the various light beams of different wavelengths arriving in the corresponding number of fibers from the individual transmitters (transmitter fibers).

Light beams emerging from the individual transmitter fibers are first collimated by a lens before striking the reflection diffraction grating at an oblique angle to the optical axis. The grating reflects the light in a specific direction in accordance with its colour, i.e. wavelength. The lens converts the directional change (angular dispersion) into a local displacement of the image point. The image points of all wavelengths coincide at a single point if the characteristics of the grating and the lens, as well as the angle of inclination of the grating in relation to the optical axis and the position of the transmitter fibers, are properly chosen. Finally, the mixture of wavelengths is coupled into the transmission fiber at the point where they coincide.

The transmission fiber has a fixed core diameter of 50 μm and an outside diameter of 125 μm. If such fibers were also used as transmitter fibers, the result would be extremely narrow spectral passband widths of no more than a few nanometers. This in turn would result in extremely high coupling losses from LED light sources and in very narrow tolerances for the emission wavelengths from laser light sources. By reducing the core and outside diameters of transmitter fibers to 30 μm and 45 μm respectively, it is possible to increase the passband width to approximately 20 nm with a wavelength interval of 36 nm between individual channels. These values appear satisfactory for practical operation.

Housing structures for these multiplexers are compact, robust and permit simple adjustment (a few minutes is necessary for this). The grating comprises etched silicon wafers with 3.5 micrometer groove

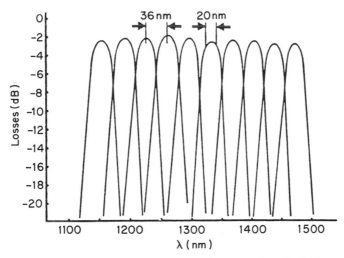

Fig. 3.11 Typical optical transmission response for a wavelength division multiplexer (WDM) (with grateful acknowledgment to AEG of West Germany from whose published product information this figure was taken with permission).

spacings and with a chromium-gold layer evaporated to form the reflecting surface — all conventional silicon-chip technology and therefore low-cost production.

Ten-channel multiplexers of this type are readily produced, having typically 36 nm channel spacing and a pass bandwidth of 20 nm (defined by the distance between the points at which the transmission loss has increased 1 dB above the attenuation in the center of the channel). The insertion loss in the center of the channel varies between 1.9 and 2.8 dB: of this value, 0.7 to 1.2 dB are due to the grating and approximately 1.0 dB to reflection losses at the fiber ends and lens.

A typical transmission response for such a multiplexer is shown in Fig. 3.11.

These types of WDM components are housed in rectangular boxes approximately 12 mm × 12 mm × 40 mm and exhibit typically 0.2 dB insertion loss variations over the − 20 to + 60 °C temperature range.

One example of WDM component application is in West Germany's BIGFON networks.

Amphenol supply a single-mode coupler that multiplexes two signals: 1300 nm and 1500 nm. The maximum excess loss is 0−5 dB and the isolation is 20 dB over a 20-nm bandwidth.

Corning-France have announced a WDM product operating on 850 nm and 1300 nm. This product has an insertion loss of 1.5 dB and an isolation of 30 dB. Other products such as duplexers using this monolithic technology are under advanced development.

3.5   OPTICAL MULTIPLEXING: SYSTEMS ASPECTS

The arrangement shown in Fig. 3.12 is sometimes called space-division multiplexing or SDM.

Since fibers are relatively small and light (and the transmitter and receiver can have similar advantages) this method is rather more cost

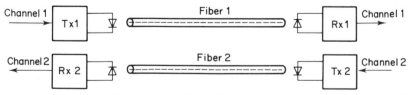

Fig. 3.12   Multiplexing by means of physically separate channels (sometimes referred to as 'space division multiplexing').

effective in practice than it may appear on paper. Therefore this simple two-fiber approach is often used.

As already described optical multiplexing is used for fiber multichannelling or sometimes for duplexing (simultaneous transmission and reception on one fiber).

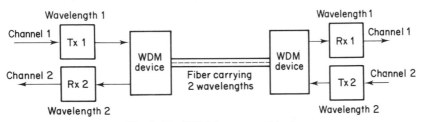

Fig. 3.13   WDM : system block.

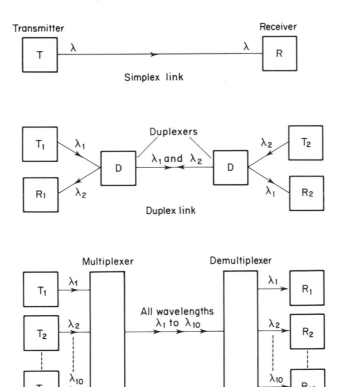

Example: 10 - channel multiplexer link

Fig. 3.14   Simplex, duplex and ten-channel multiplex links. (In all these diagrams λ refers to wavelength.)

A 2-channel duplex WDM system arrangement is shown in Fig. 3.13.

The WDM devices separate, by changing the directions of light at different wavelengths, the channels at the appropriate transmitters (Tx) and receivers (Rx). Problems to be addressed regarding the future of WDM include: the reliability of the overall system with only one fiber, the fact that fiber characteristics are strictly matched to specific wavelengths, the losses, and the unit prices of WDM devices.

It is possible to obtain WDM devices that will multiplex and de-multiplex up to about ten separate channels as shown in the third system block of Fig. 3.14.

4

Electro-optic modules

4.1 TRANSMITTERS: LEDs AND LASERS

4.1.1 LEDs (light-emitting diodes)

These optical sources are frequently encountered in short-to-moderate range links, including most electro-optic modules where such are used in local networks (e.g. 'LANs').

More familiar examples of LEDs include visible display devices used on equipment such as clocks, stereos, car dashboards, etc, producing visible light of several possible colours: red, orange, yellow or green.

The basic principles of operation of LEDs for optical fiber communications are identical to those applying to the simpler (and generally cheaper) display devices. For LEDs intended for use with fibers, however, the operating wavelengths are carefully chosen (designed-in) and several other features are made specially compatible with efficiently launching power into a fiber.

The optical power levels available from LEDs are low relative to those obtainable from lasers.

A LED is a form of (semiconductor) microchip which inherently produces optical output for electrical input.

LEDs for optical fiber systems often just show some red light, but most of their output lies in the near infra-red (i.r.). This is because, as explained in Chapter 2, fibers yield lowest power losses at certain wavelengths in the near or towards the middle i.r. (there are other advantages also). The dominant wavelengths emitted depend upon the materials chosen for the LED and their precise combination.

Silicon — the material of nearly all conventional microchips — is unsuitable for LEDs; very little light will be emitted because silicon is extremely inefficient at converting electrical energy into light.

Gallium arsenide (GaAs) is efficient, especially when certain other materials are added, such as aluminum, germanium or phosphorus.

With LEDs three basic types of design exist: the 'Burrus' diode structure, the micro-lensed or 'sweet spot' (trade name due to Honeywell) devices and edge-emitting devices (ELEDs). The Burrus structure has been available for several years but is not frequently used in modern systems (Fig. 4.1).

More recently, technology has advanced to the state where it is possible, under production conditions, to place a microscopic glass bead that acts as a lens on top of the diode's microchip structure. This 'sweet spot' micro-lensed device has the advantage of direct compatibility with a very wide range of possible fibers. Double-lensed

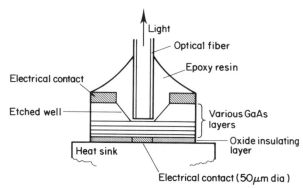

Fig. 4.1   The Burrus (or 'double-heterostructure') LED.

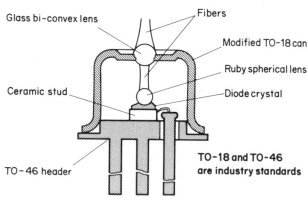

Fig. 4.2   A double-lensed LED-based transmitter structure.

versions (Fig. 4.2) allow the light to be concentrated into the output fiber 'pigtail'.

Most of the available Burrus and sweet-spot LEDs cost only a few dollars ($1–10 range) and offer high reliability long-term operation.

Edge-emitting LEDs are designed with very small emission regions. This allows much faster operation (beyond 140 Mbit/s) but at lower output power and therefore these 'ELEDs' are restricted to shorter range applications.

Dominant wavelengths

Many LEDs will have a maximum power at a dominant wavelength lying somewhere within the range 800 to 850 nm. Some LEDs are available for other wavelengths: either around 1300 nm (2nd 'window') or around 1550 nm (3rd 'window').

The choice is dictated by:

(1) 'Windows', i.e. loss minima, in fibers;
(2) Availability of suitable detectors;
(3) Cost;
(4) Minimization of pulse-spreading in a fiber;
(5) Reliability considerations.

The facility for wavelength-division multiplexing (WDM: see Chapter 3.4) can also be a factor influencing choice.

Spectral link width

This is another parameter strongly affecting applications. The curve of relative (optical) power against wavelength (Fig. 4.3) shows how this is defined.

It is important to ensure that the spectral line width is kept fairly small — to concentrate power at the peak and to achieve item (4) on the list above — although the use of really narrow line width sources (e.g. lasers) is not recommended for multimode fibers. Therefore LEDs tend to be used in systems where multimode fibers are installed.

Output power

Obviously this must be maximized — bearing in mind the other parameters also. However, the quoted output power of the device does not

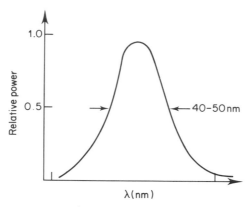

Fig. 4.3 Optical power spectrum of a typical LED.

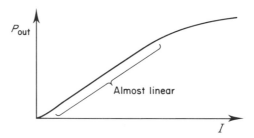

Fig. 4.4 Optical power as a function of electrical drive current for a typical LED.

mean much since we are only interested in the power actually coupled into the fiber.

The LED itself might for example conceivably output 1 mW. But the coupling-efficiency, from LED to fiber, could be as low as 40%. This would mean that only 400 μW is actually entering the fiber at the transmitting end. This type of situation is quite representative of several higher-powered LEDs.

Throughout much of its operating range, the optical output power (P_{out}) of a LED is almost directly proportional — linearly related — to the electrical input current (I) as indicated in Fig. 4.4.

In a system any non-linearity of the source is manifested as *distortion* of the signal (during source modulation).

Such distortion is a particularly serious problem where an *analog* modulation scheme is recommended and leads to the choice, usually, of FM rather than AM for optical transmission. This is because AM demands high linearity.

A typical FM waveform (the output optical power) was shown in Chapter 1. Only the waveform mid-point crossings, 'zero-crossings' for a.c., are required to be regularly detected and this process is relatively insensitive to non-linearities.

Spatial distribution of emitted light

Light produced by any LED does not project in an ideal collimated (parallel) beam but rather spreads out. This results in the coupling efficiency feature already mentioned — only a certain amount of the light can ever enter the fiber as required. Lensed ('sweet spot') devices considerably alleviate this problem.

For the fastest LEDs, operating into small-diameter fibers, finer structures known as edge-emitting are required. Generally these 'ELEDs' cannot produce so much power as other devices but recently a few milliwatts of power have been launched into fibers by commercially available ELEDs. Such devices attract higher unit prices than is the case for LEDs such as 'sweet spot'.

Modulation rates and output power

At relatively low modulation rates, usually up to a few tens of MHz, LEDs can produce their full output power. As the modulation rate is increased towards 100 MHz the output power steadily falls.

Modulation of a LED, or other optical transmitter is shown schematically in Fig. 4.5. The modulating driver provides sufficient power at suitable voltage levels to efficiently drive the LED.

There is an important modulation bandwidth/output power trade-off for any given LED: either we have higher output power but lower modulation rate, or vice versa.

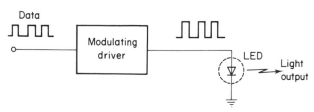

Fig. 4.5 The principle of modulating a LED by direct electronic means (as opposed to external optical modulation.

Typical power/frequency curves are shown in the graph of Fig. 4.6 for three different LEDs. Higher power LEDs are generally slower than lower power LEDs.

Linearization of LED output power/current characteristic

Substantial progress has been made in linearizing the output of LEDs for multichannel analog transmission. One technique is shown in Fig. 4.7.

The electrical reference channel voltage level is assumed to be kept constant. If, for example, the power from LED 1 were to fall then this, being detected by the monitor photodetector, is sensed and yields an increased error control voltage. This increased drive and hence increased output power is available from LED 2, which feeds into the coupling optical tee and therefore compensates the initial loss of power.

Improvements achieved over a single LED are:

● greater than 35 dB in second-order distortion
● greater than 20 dB in third-order distortion.

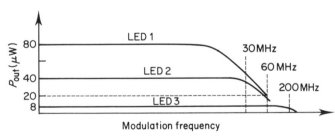

Fig. 4.6 Optical output power versus input information signal frequency (for a variety of LEDs).

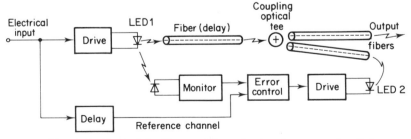

Fig. 4.7 Optical feedforward linearization for an analog link.

With this approach several TV channels may be simultaneously transmitted over at least 2 km without repeaters.

ANT (West Germany) have recently demonstrated ELED transmitters delivering 140 Mbit/s over a fiber cable up to 7 km in length, but several in the industry consider that lasers will eventually take over this type of role.

4.1.2 Semiconductor lasers

For optical systems where extremely high-speed data must be carried — hundreds of Mbit/s or even several gigabits per second — or where a more modest speed is required over relatively long distances, LEDs are unavailable and lasers are demanded. The simplest concept of a laser is an optical oscillator. In the case of a semiconductor laser an electrical input is applied to an appropriate semiconductor material junction and optical energy is built up and confined (wavelength determined) within a microscopic internal *cavity*.

When discussing LEDs we noted that the wavelengths depend mainly on the choice of materials. Similar remarks apply to lasers and, like LEDs, they are generally based on gallium arsenide semiconductors — with some additions such as aluminum. Electrical energy forms the 'stimulating' input and lasing is produced by a build-up of light energy due to multiple reflections between mirrors. One mirror is slightly less reflecting than the other and the laser light, at a power of typically a few milliwatts, is focused out of this mirror-end. This arrangement forms the internal cavity. Researchers are achieving about one-tenth of a watt of continuous laser power from sophisticated versions of such devices. New laser developments occur at frequent intervals and examples of active organizations are:

- Bell Telephone,
- Plessey,
- Fujitsu.

In external appearance a laser looks very much like a LED. But the internal construction, and power supply, are much more complex than those required for a LED. This leads to considerably greater unit prices, typically to several hundred dollars for a laser. (But unit prices are falling.)

Dominant wavelengths

The operating wavelengths of semiconductor lasers are similar to those applicable to LEDs. With some lasers a degree of electronic tunability is available.

Spectral line width

This is generally around or less than 1/20th that of a LED and can sometimes be as small as 0.01 nm for commercially available lasers. A basic output power spectrum for a multimode laser is shown in Fig. 4.8.

The much narrower line width of a semiconductor laser means greatly reduced dispersion in the fiber (Chapter 2). It also enables WDM to be considered.

These transmitter devices are almost always used with single-mode fibers.

Semiconductor laser manufacture requires complex semiconductor fabrication processes and two types are shown in Fig. 4.9. In each case the various layers are, for short-wavelength lasers, various compounds of gallium arsenide and aluminum. (With the exceptions of the final metallic — usually aluminum — electrical contacts and the silicon dioxide insulator in the BH case.) For long-wavelength lasers, 1300 nm and longer, compounds of indium and phosphorus are combined with the gallium arsenide; but the structural layouts remain identical to those shown in Fig. 4.9.

These buried heterostructures (BH) offer improvements over simpler laser structures, making the increased manufacturing complexity worth pursuing. With BH or MSBH devices, stripe widths as small as 2 μm have been produced and threshold currents of less than 10 mA have been obtained. Although this limits the total optical output to usually below 2 mW, such lasers show better temporal stability and greater

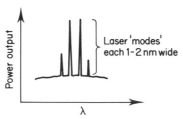

Fig. 4.8 Basic output power spectrum for a multimode semiconductor laser.

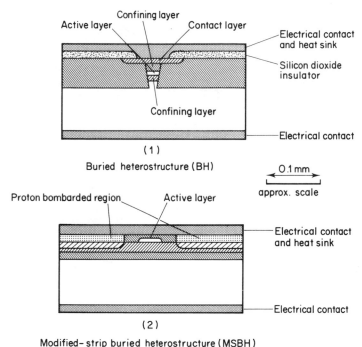

Fig. 4.9 Simplified cross-sections of 'buried heterostructure' semiconductor lasers.

linearity of output power/input electrical current characteristics than simpler structures. It is also easier to operate such lasers in a single 'longitudinal' mode. For these reasons they have become important for fiber-optic communications systems.

The MSBH structure, requiring proton-bombarded semiconductor regions, avoids the otherwise rather awkward silicon dioxide insulator of the BH laser.

It is essential for the laser 'chips' to be packaged in a form acceptable to an OEM or systems house and two types of package are shown in Fig. 4.10. Electrical inputs and optical outputs are shown. Notice the heat sink for the flat package:1 W or more of heat often has to be dissipated.

Modern lasers can be supplied with internal optical feedback resulting in monomode (or 'single-mode') operation. A power spectrum such as that shown in Fig. 4.11 results. Notice that the line width of the principal and dominant mode is much less than 1 nm.

The spectral line width contrasts become apparent when a laser

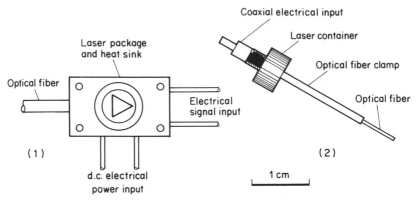

Fig. 4.10 Semiconductor laser diode packages of the flat (1) and coaxial (2) configurations.

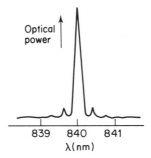

Fig. 4.11 A typical spectral characteristic of a single-mode short-wavelength semiconductor laser.

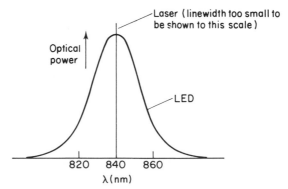

Fig. 4.12 Overlay comparison of single-mode laser and LED spectra.

spectrum is shown together with that of a LED, to the same scale (Fig. 4.12).

Some further comparative aspects of semiconductor lasers are next considered.

Output power

This is generally well above the power obtainable from a LED. Up to 100 mW or so is possible and over 10 mW coupled into the fiber is quite typical for modern production devices.

Spatial distribution of emitted light

This is much narrower, better collimated, than for a LED and higher coupling efficiency to the fiber results.

Modulation rates

A laser can be modulated at a much faster rate than a LED due to a major effect in their basic operation, called 'stimulated emission'.

A modulating driver is employed, like the scheme shown in Fig. 4.5, for the LED, but this is generally more complex for driving a laser. Some modern lasers with several mW of output power can be modulated at rates exceeding 10 Gbit/s.

It is possible to externally modulate the light using devices such as electro-optic modulators, but the advantage common to both lasers and LEDs is the ability to modulate directly by applying an electrical input.

All laser power-current characteristics exhibit an initial low-power level regime, prior to the onset of lasing. Once lasing has commenced further increases in current are followed by steady (*linear* — in modern lasers) increases in optical output power.

Unit prices

Typical LED and laser component unit prices have been mentioned in the foregoing descriptions.

Generally unit price levels (late 1980s) may be summarized thus:

- LEDs: several dollars, $20–50 for fairly high-speed devices.
- Lasers: upwards of $200.

Complete LED-based transmitter modules may be obtained for about $50 or somewhat less (to some tens of Kbit/s modulation rates).

More sophisticated units operable at rates up to some Mbit/s cost generally over $200.

Laser-based transmitter modules cost from several hundred up to over a thousand dollars apiece.

Unit prices for electro-optic modules are currently falling and are forecast to continue to fall for several years.

Table 4.1 Summary of LEDs and lasers

	Power into fiber (mW)	Spectral line width	Analog sign-alling band-width	Max. trans-mission speed (bits/s)
LEDs	0.1 to 1 (less for an ELED at 140 Mbit/s)	Rather broad	Rather narrow	Some 200 million or so
Semiconductor lasers[1]	2 to 50 cw production (100 research)	Very narrow	Broad (e.g. several TV channels)	At least a few billion

	Tunability[2]	Com-patibility with single-mode fiber	Long wavelength operation (1300 or 1550 nm)	Life (years)	Unit price
LEDs	No	Possible but unusual	Yes	At least 100	Relatively low
Semicon-ductor lasers[1]	Can be tunable	Excellent	Yes	At least 100	Relatively high

[1] It is advisable to keep the eye 10 cm or more distant from laser-produced radiation. Safety can be a serious problem with semiconductor lasers (as with *any* laser).
[2] This means the ability to electronically select wavelengths (e.g. for optimizing to the transmission fiber).

4.2 RECEIVERS: PIN, PIN-FET AND APD PHOTODETECTORS

4.2.1 Initial consideration

At the receiving end of a fiber transmission system, a photodetector converts optical power to an electric current. The requirements of suitable photodetectors are:

- high sensitivity at the wavelength of the optical carrier (e.g. 800, 1300 or 1550 nm)
- sufficient bandwidth to cope with the desired information rate
- low noise performance
- stable characteristics
- size compatible with fiber dimensions
- low cost.

The wavelength of operation is dictated by the device material.

Silicon is best for shorter wavelengths (800–900 nm), germanium for moderate wavelengths (1300 nm), indium gallium arsenide for longer wavelengths (1550 nm).

The unit price generally rises greatly with indium gallium arsenide detectors.

4.2.2 Responsivity

There is a precise parameter relating to the photodetector diode material itself — responsivity (R).

This is the electric current I_p resulting from a specified optical power P_{opt}.

$$R = I_p / P_{opt}$$

Responsivity depends upon the optical wavelength, diode efficiency, and various fundamental constraints.

Responsivity units are: A/W (amps/watt) or $\mu A/\mu W$.

Typical values of responsivity, and cost comparisons, are given in Table 4.2.

Table 4.2 Responsivity and cost

	Silicon 800 nm	Germanium 1300 nm	Indium gallium arsenide 1300 nm
Responsivity	0.6	0.5	0.6
Cost (relative)	fairly low	fairly low	higher

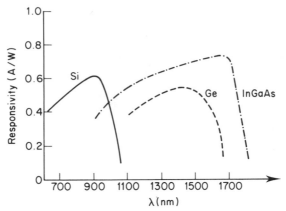

Fig. 4.13   Responsivity as a function of wavelength for a variety of semiconductor materials used in photodetector diodes.

Wavelength dependence

Responsivity varies quite strongly with wavelength. It peaks at some wavelength, depending on the actual diode, and falls both at shorter and longer wavelengths. At shorter wavelengths the diode absorbs strongly and the current developed is due to only a relatively weak effect near the surface of the diode. At longer wavelengths there is weak absorption causing excessive optical penetration through the diode. Again, only a weak current-producing effect ensues.

The curves of Fig. 4.13 summarize this situation.

In any of the materials we can realize either:

● PIN photodetector diodes

or

● avalanche photodiodes (APDs).

The PIN diode is the simpler detector but it has a lower sensitivity than the avalanche photodiode which provides internal gain via an avalanche process. However, this produces extra noise. PIN diodes are the most common and are fully compatible with LED-driven multi-mode fiber systems.

In many modern optical-fiber systems we encounter so-called 'PIN-FET' receivers. These are fully integrated units that almost optimally transfer the photoelectric output from the PIN detector on through to a pre-amplifier. PIN-FET receivers are the worldwide

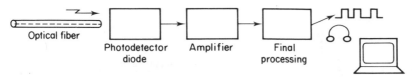

Fig. 4.14 Schematic of a 'general' fiber-optic link receiver.

standard detector units for long-wavelength systems; typical manufacturers include; AT & T, BT & D, NTT and Plessey.

For faster operation, particularly at or beyond a few Gbit/s, PIN diodes will not cope and an avalanche diode (APD) is required.

APDs are generally associated with laser-driven single-mode fiber systems and they have to be selected appropriately to suit the transmitted wavelength.

The signal energy, once converted back into electricity using either a PIN or an avalanche photodiode, is weak. In fact the amount of signal power available is similar to that encountered with satellite communications receivers: nanowatts or even picowatts (billionths or trillionths of a watt). Clearly we require substantial amplification of the signal, following the detector diode. It turns out that the first amplifier has to be rather special and of low noise capability. With LED/multimode fiber/PIN systems the first amplifying stage uses silicon microchips. In the case of laser/single-mode fiber/APD systems gallium arsenide transistor amplifiers are required to cope with the high speeds. It is possible that the entire receiver unit, APD plus amplifying and signal processing electronics, may all be on a single gallium arsenide microchip coming on to the market shortly.

After this initial processing the signal emerges as useful data, telephone channel, or TV, as indicated in Fig. 4.14.

4.2.3 Power budgets

These have already been defined (see earlier definitions) — they determine the optical power entering the photodetector diode and hence: the received signal/noise ratio and BER.

In many optical-fiber receiving systems the BER must be better than 10^{-9} and a minimum received signal power P_2 is quoted that will achieve this. The power budget may then be developed as indicated rather generally in Fig. 4.15. P_1 is the optical power actually launched

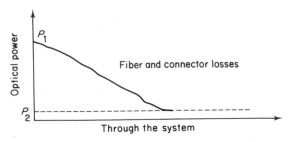

Fig. 4.15 Simplified concept of a link power budget.

into the fiber at the transmitting end and P_2 is the power available at the photodetector. Typically, P_2 might be 100 nW (– 40 dBm).

If P_1 is 100 mW (– 10 dBm) then the total allowable fiber attenuation is 40 – 10 = 30 dB.

For a fiber loss of 6 dB/km at the operating wavelength, and neglecting dispersion here, the maximum length of fiber is 5 km. We conclude that detector sensitivity (and transmitter power) determine, partly at least, link length. The minimum allowable received power is often quoted as receiver sensitivity.

4.2.4 Dynamic range

This is the maximum range of optical input signal power over which the receiver can be used and remain within specification (especially with regard to *linearity*). The minimum level is the sensitivity as defined above. The maximum is set just below the onset of severe distortion.

For data links: values will be around 30 dB for low-moderate data rates, down to 20 dB for higher data rates.

4.2.5 Speed of response

Two main features influence speed.

● transit time within the photodiode
● electrical effects of the diode ('time constant').

Electrical effects in well designed diodes can readily result in frequency restrictions, due to these effects, exceeding 1 GHz (1000 MHz). However, when we also consider the preamplifier we can easily find that — with a PIN photodiode — the bandwidth is restricted to only a few tens of MHz.

A basic diode parameter that increases responsivity also, unfortunately, increases transit time. Thus there is a trade-off between responsivity and speed. Speeds of about 0.1 ns are, however, common.

4.2.6 Noise impairments

Several sources of noise affect the reception of optical signals:

(1) background light entering the photodetector
(2) modal or 'speckle' noise (if laser driven)
(3) 'quantum' noise at the photodetector
(4) 'shot' noise at the photodetector
(5) dark current noise at the photodetector
(6) avalanche noise (if an APD is used)
(7) thermal and shot noise in the preamplifier.

Item (1) is reduced (virtually eliminated) by well-sealed fiber-detector structures. Items (3) and (5) are specific to photodetectors — dark current noise (the noise remaining when zero light enters) is one measure of detector quality. Items (4) and (7) are minimized by good electronics design.

The diagram of Fig. 4.16 represents a summary of these effects.

4.2.7 Examples for a selection of PCM systems

As remarked earlier, with digital systems (on which we shall concentrate here), the noise strongly affects the receiver bit-error rate (BER).

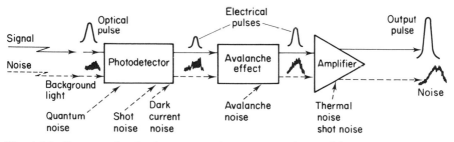

Fig. 4.16 Sources of noise in an optical receiver (with grateful acknowledgment to Y. Suematsu and K.-I. Iga from whose work *Introduction to Optical Fiber Communications* this figure was taken with their permission).

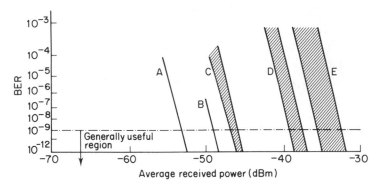

Fig. 4.17 BER as a function of average received power for five representative pulse code modulated (PCM) links (with grateful acknowledgment to Y. Suematsu and K.-I. Iga from whose work *Introduction to Optical Fiber Communications* this figure was taken with their permission).

Practical values of the BER, as a function of average received signal power, are available for PCM sent over various links. The graph of Fig. 4.17 shows the values obtained where an APD is used.

On the graph the letter notation refers to the following.

A: Multimode graded-index, 32 Mbit/s over 1.4 km.
B: Multimode step-index, 32 Mbit/s over 1 km.
C: Multimode graded-index, 100 Mbit/s over 2–8 km.
D: Single-mode, 400 Mbit/s over 2–5 km.
E: Multimode graded-index, 400 Mbit/s over 1–4 km.

As an example, taking the group of curves C, the received signal must exceed − 46 dBm if the BER is to remain below 10^{-9} for a 100 Mbit/s moderate-range link using multimode graded-index fiber.

With PIN photodiodes thermal noise usually dominates. Calculations show that increasing the effective load resistance on the diode will allow the range to be increased without sacrificing the signal-to-noise ratio (i.e. use FET or MOS transistor circuits). However, the speed of response will be degraded unless special circuit designs are implemented to compensate ('equalization'). There are limits to this approach.

APDs will accept extremely low minimum detectable optical power (from about 10^{-2} picowatts to 10 nanowatts; − 110 dBm to − 50 dBm, depending on bandwidth). This in spite of the noise problems existing with all receivers. Also, APD response remains linear over many orders of magnitude of this incident optical power. (Drawbacks of APDs include stability problems, requirement for a relatively high d.c. supply voltage, and higher cost.)

Interpretation: Use PIN photodetectors (PIN-FETs preferably) whenever possible.

4.3   TRANSMITTER AND RECEIVER MODULES, TRANSCEIVERS AND MODEMS

Transmitter or receiver modules for fiber-optic systems generally use linear integrated circuits (IC) within their structure.

Typically, the LED or laser, the PIN or APD photodiode, or the PIN-FET arrangement, are combined with the modulator or pre-amplifier in at least a hybrid IC module.

A large number of manufacturers offer these types of products, originating from the USA, Japan, the UK and mainland Europe.

The overall physical size of such a unit is typically that of any more conventional all-electronic IC based module. D.c. power requirements must be considered, and are:

- relatively simple and straightforward where a PIN photo-detector is used (unless a laser is also incorporated)
- much more elaborate where an APD is used since relatively high voltages, e.g. 40 to 110 V, are essential.

PIN-FET receivers typically operate with input optical power levels of only some tens of nW and data rates up to 565 Mbit/s.

Such receivers are usually hybrid-integrated within metallized housings about 20 mm × 10 mm × 5 mm in dimensions.

Optical-fiber connector ports vary, e.g. the *de facto* standard SMA, or ST, etc (see Chapter 3).

Table 4.3 indicates typical performance data for integrated fiber-optic transmitter and receiver modules operating at bit rates up to 220 Mbit/s and at the second window wavelength (1320 nm).

Table 4.3 Typical performance of integrated fiber-optic transmitter and receiver modules

Transmitter	
Supply voltage	+ 5 V or − 5.2 V
Power dissipation	500 mW
Input data rate	1 to 220 Mbit/s
Average output power	− 17 dBm into 62.5/125/0.29 fiber
	− 22 dBm into 50/125/0.2 fiber
Center wavelength	1320 nm
LED spectral width	110 nm
Receiver	
Supply voltage	+ 5 V or − 5.2 V
Power dissipation	250 mW
Sensitivity	− 35 dBm (1 Mbit/s), − 37 dBm (5 to 125 Mbit/s), − 35 dBm (220 Mbit/s)
Dynamic range	20 dB

The data in this table applies to modules suitable for LAN or local loop applications. ICs within the modules process the digital signals.

4.4 FIBER-OPTIC MODEMS: TRANSCEIVERS

Conventional (electrical) modems MODulate the signal on one frequency and DEModulate generally on a different frequency, i.e. coherent (frequency conscious) operation occurs. This is *not* the case with modems for fiber optic systems since these are required to interface an electrical bus (e.g. RS 232C) with transmit and receive fibers.

Within each modem there is thus a transmitter and a receiver, i.e. often a LED and a PIN-FET arrangement — assuming a multimode-fiber link within the system. Such modules are essentially *transceivers*.

An optical fiber connects between each transmitter and receiver. Information signals (data, PCM voice, etc) are fed electrically to and from the local modems, often using a standard RS 232C interface as shown in Fig. 4.18.

Although the data rates may be quite low, perhaps 4800 or 9000 bit/s, high-speed data transfer is only one advantage of fiber

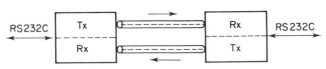

Fig. 4.18 Block diagram of a fiber-optic modem.

optics (i.e. such systems may take advantage of the inherent freedom from interference offered, for example).

These modems come ready supplied with both fiber optic and electrical connector ports.

Complete terminal units (telephone exchanges, computer terminals or workstations, etc) are sometimes available with such modems fitted as standard. Otherwise retrofitting may be required where a system is to be upgraded using fiber optics.

Some manufacturers now offer transceivers typically operating at 40 Mbit/s that code, decode, provide transmission and reception all combined in one module. Used in a digital telephone exchange, for example, such technology can reduce the overall size of the exchange unit to one-seventh of the original size — without such transceivers. Typical dimensions for such modules are 70 mm × 40 mm × 11 mm.

4.5 FACTORS INFLUENCING UNIT PRICES

These include:

- bit-rate requirements;
- transmitter power/receiver sensitivity;
- module complexity;
- quantity purchased.

It is generally true to say that module unit prices rise with:

- increase in bit rate;
- increase in transmitter power/receiver sensitivity;
- increase in module complexity;
- decrease in quantity purchased.

(For example: a 140 Mbit/s module will cost more to purchase than a 10 Mbit/s version — even assuming all other factors constant.)

Some examples will give guidance regarding the typical unit prices of receivers. An IC receiver (without photodetector) attracting a unit price of about $20 will typically provide: 20 MHz capability, or 15 Mbit/s NRZ data extendable to 50 Mbit/s; TTL and CMOS compatibility. When a PIN photodetector plus other extra required components are added the total unit price becomes about $30.

In contrast, receivers capable of handling data up to a rate of 200 Kbit/s can be purchased for around $8.

4.6 MODULATION

Occasionally this may be analog, e.g. for speech or TV signals in the form of AM or FM; or some variant, generally related to FM.

More often digital modulation is required for data transmission or for handling digitized speech or TV. In this way linearity problems are essentially avoided and it should also be remembered that digitally-modulated systems are the basis of the current convergence trend between computers and communications.

Hardware for digital electronic technology is readily obtainable, often in VLSI chip form and is relatively inexpensive at low to moderate bit rates.

The simplest digital modulation scheme to consider is Non-Return-to-Zero-Level (NRZ-L) coding; often referred to as the 'baseband NRZ-L data' and indicated by the electrical waveforms shown in Fig. 4.19.

In operation, this simple NRZ-L pattern is subject to a serious problem. Baseline wander can occur after a long sequence of zeros, and subsequently data can be lost. Scrambling and modulo -2 addition can alleviate this problem but the NRZ encoding and decoding becomes complex.

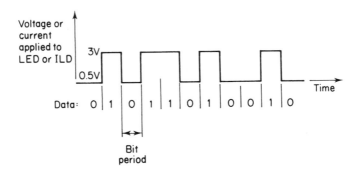

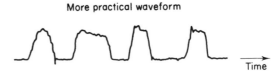

Fig. 4.19 Examples of NRZ-L waveforms.

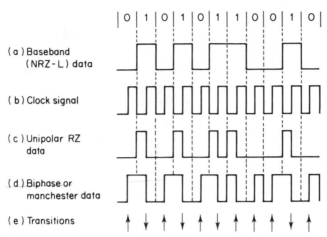

Fig. 4.20 A synchronous comparison between a selection of digital modulation schemes (with grateful acknowledgment to G. Keiser from whose work *Optical Fiber Communications*, published by McGraw-Hill, this figure was taken with permission).

Rz codes

With these codes each data bit is encoded as two optical code bits. This requires more bandwidth than NRZ but plenty of bandwidth is generally available with fiber.

Examples are shown by the waveforms of Fig. 4.20.

Unipolar RZ data suffers another drawback associated with long strings of zeros in the data, namely loss of timing synchronization in the receiver.

Manchester code avoids this problem because transitions then occur even between zeros. The optical Manchester code is unipolar (we can only have optical power *on* or *off*, not reverse, and this code is sometimes called 'Manchester − II'. It is easy to generate Manchester code by modulo − 2 adding the NRZ-L and clock waves. The maximum data speed is now the same as that of the clock — although the final *bit rate* is identical to the original 'baseband' bit rate.

Block codes are also sometimes used. These, at the expense of increased bandwidth, provide adequate timing and error-monitoring information as well as eliminating long strings of ones or zeros. (These basically amount to redundant binary codes, deliberately transmitting more bits than actually present in the information, according to some format.)

One such block code is 4B/5B. With the 4B/5B scheme encoding proceeds by taking blocks of four bits (a nibble) and this results in more spectrally efficient modulation than, for example, Manchester. At 100 Mbit/s Manchester code requires 200 MHz modulation capability of the transmitters and a similar detection capability for the (PIN-FET) receivers. Contrastingly, the 4B/5B code demands only a 125 MHz modulation rate.

Another code used in fiber-optic systems is termed the HSB3 ('high speed bipolar 3'). This is often alternatively referred to as HDB3 ('high density bipolar 3'). It is a *three-level* code that allows connection to a ternary channel.

For each binary 'zero': send continuous signal at zero level. (Except, for every block of *four* zeros a specific pulse sequence is transmitted.)

For each binary 'one': send alternating positive and negative pulses of half-bit duration.

In the optical system this means transmitting three distinct levels of optical power.

HDB3 is now an important CCITT standard code.

Finally, we will mention code-mark-inversion (CMI). Again, half-bit period pulses are used. For binary 'zero' the signal 01 is generated (using the inverse of the clock); for every binary 'one' alternate full-bit high-level signals are sent.

4.7   TIME-DIVISION MULTIPLEXERS (TDM 'MUX' UNITS)

In any multi-way and/or multi-terminal system devices are required to combine several channels of information. The devices concerned are multiplexers and they are found in many electrical and optical networks. It is important to distinguish between 'temporal' and optical multiplexing. Optical multiplexers include the WDM units described earlier. Most temporal multiplexers ('MUX') perform time-division-multiplexing (TDM) and they operate internally in an electrical mode. Each electrical input channel originates from a terminal and comprises conventional addressed and coded data streams. The data rate will

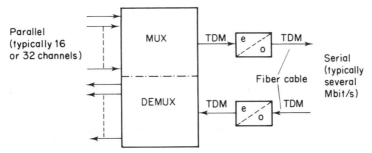

Fig. 4.21   Time-division multiplexer (TDM) MUX/DEMUX with electro-optic (e/o)
interfaces.

typically be some Kbit/s (i.e. a few thousand baud). Within the
multiplexer these data streams are identified and assembled into one
new fast serial stream. The parallel channels may operate at 4800 or
9600 bit/s whereas the serial data streams are likely to have bit rates
between 1 and 100 Mbit/s or even higher.

A block diagram of a TDM multiplexer is given in Fig. 4.21.

The unit shown in the diagram is fairly typical of an optical system
multiplexer, although not all available units need to handle up to 32
channels. There are as many demultiplexed output channels as original
input channels and the TDM data streams are read to and from the
fibers via optoelectronic modules.

All the multiplexing and demultiplexing is performed electrically.
Twisted wire pair cables, or flat *ribbon cables*, are adequate for the
parallel data channels while fiber cables are used for TDM serial
transmission.

There are a number of manufacturers worldwide of these types of
units.

5

Cable TV, closed-circuit TV and financial services systems

5.1 FIBER OPTICS IN CABLE TV

5.1.1 Introductory points

To date fiber optics has achieved only limited penetration in cable TV systems, with the exception of the USA and Japan. Conventional coaxial copper cable systems satisfy many of the criteria required, for example:

- One-way (subscriber) off-air or locally distributed programs.
- It is well understood, easily branched for installation, and easily soldered.
- There is no need for electro-optic conversion.

Factors that may serve to increase the penetration of fiber optics include the substantially greater bandwidth and distance associated with this medium, well beyond coaxial cable capabilities. There is the impact of EMC standards which will exert pressure on the use of the new medium with its inherent EMI immunity.

One example of a service demanding increased bandwidth is high-definition TV (HDTV) which is under advanced development for the consumer, particularly in Japan (Sony) and Western Europe (Philips). The HDTV market is expected to amount to about $100 billion worldwide by year 2000.

Trunk sections of any system represent the initial opportunity for fiber-optic implementation and we now consider some technical aspects of a typical trunk section implemented (as for most current systems) in analog form.

FM, or some variant thereof, is generally used and an example of a relatively simple system based on four such FM carriers, F1, F2, F3 and F4, is shown in Fig. 5.1. Typically the carrier frequencies are each a few tens of MHz and such a trunk or superprimary link can extend beyond 25 km. The transmitter is often a 1300 nm laser and the receiver a hybrid PIN-FET circuit, interconnected by single-mode optical fiber.

Primary links present a less demanding problem due mainly to their

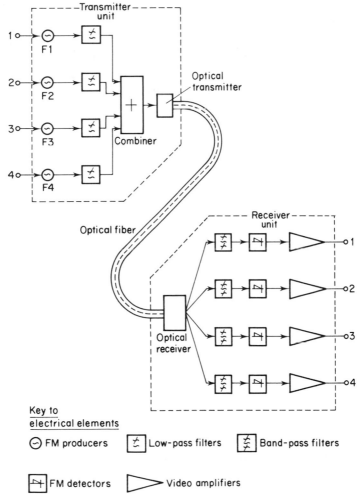

Fig. 5.1 Example of a basic four-channel fiber-optic cable TV trunk line.

shorter lengths — a few km. Graded-index multimode fibers may be used here, interconnecting 1300 nm high-radiance edge-emitting LEDs (ELEDs) and hybrid PIN-FET receivers. The final link in the system is to each individual consumer and is usually the most cost-sensitive part of the system. Miniaturization, low-cost and compatibility with FM radio broadcast channels are all desirable. Adequate reception of the FM signals, in the band 88 to 104 MHz, demands an optical receiver power comparable with that required by the TV channels. These constraints have been met by optical systems and, typically, two color TV channels plus three FM radio channels have been received with good quality using an 850 nm LED transmitter, a link several hundred meters long and PIN-photodetector receiver.

A substantial number of companies operate in various countries with business covering several aspects of cable TV and their number increases each year. Some, AT & T, British Telecom and NKF Kabel for example, are already actively involved in optical-fiber based CATV. With the unit price ($ per km) of single-mode fiber cable currently similar to that of graded index multimode, systems are tending to comprise all single-mode in many cases.

5.1.2   The British Telecom (UK) Westminster switched-star CATV system

The term 'switched-star' is applied to cable TV networks that provide an individual feed to each customer from a star point where there is a switch that routes the chosen channel to the customer's link. This system contrasts with the traditional tree and branch network, which simply distributes all the available programs on the same signal feed to each customer.

A good example of a switched-star CATV system, that has a substantial fiber-optic content, is furnished by British Telecom's (BT plc, UK) Westminster scheme. This is designed to pass 73 000 homes and 14 000 businesses, and the final configuration will have seven, or possibly eight, hubs and provide not just standard broadcast TV channels but also individual video and information services dedicated to particular customers who have the ability for substantial interaction with the system.

Program material is distributed out to the network from the head-end and since this serves a substantial geographical area of 87 000 or more customers, the first superprimary links are relatively long. A length of up to 15 km has been installed thus far, though undoubtedly there will be future applications where longer links will be needed. Fiber optics are therefore ideal for these links.

The basic trunk layout is shown for a typical section of the Westminster scheme in Fig. 5.2. From the transmission point of view the hub-site is mostly a fan-out point from where the material is sent out over the next stage, the primary links. In some configurations, however, it is possible that the hubs will also act as the source for dedicated video services (e.g. video libraries). The primaries are shorter, typically no more than 5 km, a distance that fiber optics can manage comfortably without repeaters whereas a coaxial link would need at least one. However, coaxial technology still has some advantages over its fiber-optic counterpart at present and so, despite the need for extra repeaters, the initial cost of a coaxial solution is little different. The advantage currently perceived of choosing optical transmission for these primary links is therefore confined to the long-term one of less expensive maintenance, since there is no equipment housed underground along a route.

A particular feature to note with the primary links is the extensive use of optical splitters. Many of the links are short enough to have optical power to spare. Hence those links carrying the broadcast channels (required by every switch point) can be split two or more ways. This of course saves some fiber, but more importantly it shares out the cost of the optical transmitters.

Only eight of the 10 fibers entering each WSP actually carry TV channels; the remainder carry digital controls and data.

The Wideband Switch Point (WSP) is typically a cabinet in the street with control and switching equipment for up to 300 customers. From it emanate the secondary links, carrying to each customer two TV channels (which can be selected from any of those available at the switch point), plus the FM radio band and two-way signalling. This is presently implemented as a coaxial link on grounds of cost, since it has a reach of 500 m which can cover the great majority of homes. Such a link is entirely adequate for the services provided to the customer; indeed it has spare spectrum space for future enhancements of an extra TV channel, return video channel, high speed data, etc. However there are reasons why a fiber-optic link would be preferred if it could be made cost competitive. First, reach could be extended to 1 km or more, covering all homes even in less densely populated areas. Secondly the

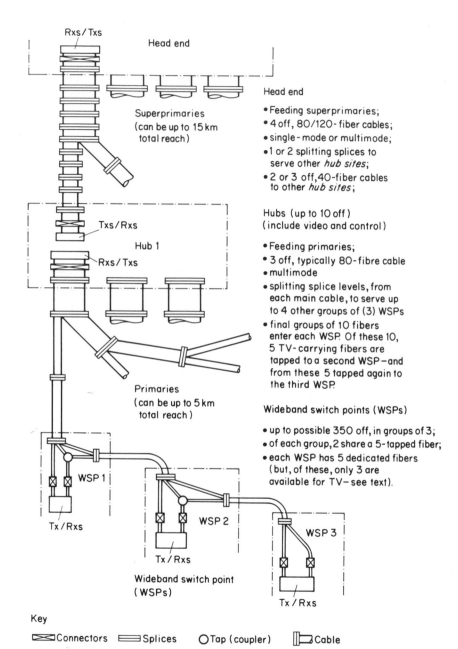

Rxs/Txs

Head end

Superprimaries
(can be up to 15 km
total reach)

Txs/Rxs

Hub 1

Rxs/Txs

Primaries
(can be up to 5 km
total reach)

WSP 1

Tx/Rxs

WSP 2

Tx/Rxs

Wideband switch point
(WSPs)

WSP 3

Tx/Rxs

Head end

• Feeding superprimaries;
• 4 off, 80/120- fiber cables;
• single-mode or multimode;
• 1 or 2 splitting splices to
  serve other *hub sites*;
• 2 or 3 off, 40-fiber cables
  to other *hub sites*;

Hubs (up to 10 off)
(include video and control)

• Feeding primaries;
• 3 off, typically 80-fibre cable
• multimode
• splitting splice levels, from
  each main cable, to serve up
  to 4 other groups of (3) WSPs
• final groups of 10 fibers
  enter each WSP. Of these 10,
  5 TV-carrying fibers are
  tapped to a second WSP—and
  from these 5 tapped again to
  the third WSP.

Wideband switch points (WSPs)

• up to possible 350 off, in groups of 3;
• of each group, 2 share a 5-tapped fiber;
• each WSP has 5 dedicated fibers
  (but, of these, only 3 are
  available for TV—see text).

Key

▧▨Connectors   ⬭Splices   ◯Tap (coupler)   ▯▢Cable

Fig. 5.2 Main configuration of the British Telecom (BT) switched-star cable TV
system, showing trunk links.

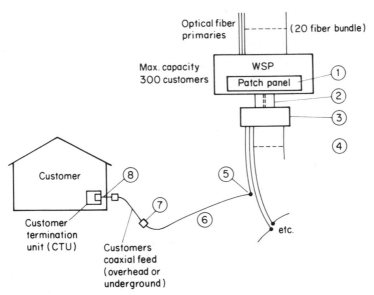

Fig. 5.3 Secondary links and customer connections associated with BT's switched-star cable TV system (numbers on the diagram refer to all-metallic sections).

smaller cables would save significantly on ducts. Thirdly it would eliminate interference problems and would automatically give the required electrical isolation between the network and equipment in the home.

The Westminster network uses only multimode fiber since no reach within the network is of sufficient length to warrant single-mode. However, it is understood that BT are investigating the possible advantages of single-mode for other schemes. In the British Telecom switched-star system mechanical jointing ('splicing') has been adopted in order to keep costs down — at least in the customer's link. Connectors remain something of a problem considering their significant losses of usually more than 1 dB regardless of the type chosen. A more practical view of those parts of the system concerned with the secondary and customer links is shown in Fig. 5.3.

In the fiber-optic sections transmitters and receivers follow very much the choices referred to earlier for the four-channel CATV system. 1.6 mW laser diodes drive the supertrunks.

The services offered on BT's Westminster network, and typical of many advanced CATV networks, include:

(1) Off-air TV and radio;

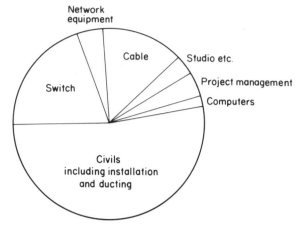

Fig. 5.4 Typical shares of system cost elements in cable TV systems.

(2) Satellite channels;
(3) Local channels;
(4) Subscription channels;
(5) Pay-as-you-watch;
(6) Interactive information services;
(7) Data transfer;
(8) On-demand interactive video.

Items (6) and (8) effectively make this system more than just conventional CATV.

A representative pie-chart indicating the shares of total CATV system costs taken by various items and aspects is given in Fig. 5.4. Note the dominance of civils, followed by switching and cable.

In most systems, CATV and others, civils invariably either dominate or take a large share of the costs, usually ranging between about 40 and 60%.

5.1.3 *French networks*

In France there has been a major initiative regarding fiber-optic CATV networks, lasting until mid-1987 in full strength (Mission Cable), although the French administration of the late 1980s initiated a substantial slowing of this program.

Analog FM lines are overlaid on networks which carry telephony, digital data and videotex. In 1983, after a change in the law affecting TV distribution, the construction of CATV networks started with two systems: switched-star with optical distribution, and limited-reach tree and branch topology coaxial. Both types of system use fiber-optic

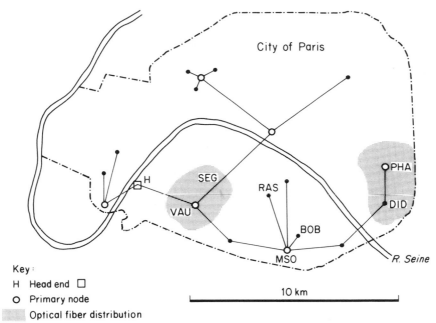

Fig. 5.5 Topology of 'super-primaries' in the Paris (France) fiber cable TV networks.

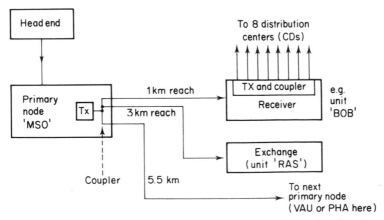

Fig. 5.6 Example of a trunk network in the Paris system outlined in Fig. 5.5.

trunks; the architecture regarding these trunks being typified by the Paris scheme shown in Figs. 5.5 and 5.6. The target specifications are presented in Table 5.1, and the French company SAT supply electro-optic subsystems to meet this specification.

Table 5.1   Example of target specification for the Paris network

	At the exchange	At the CATV hub	Subscribers outlet (baseband)	CCIR A567
Amplitude of signals (dB)	±0.5	±0.7	±2	±0.5
S/N weighted 5 MHz (dB)	56	54	48	53 (99% of time)
Linear distortion field (%)	±3	±5	±10	±6
line (%)	±3	±5	±10	±3
Amplitude/frequency (dB)	±0.5	±0.8	±1	±1
Differential gain (%)	±3	±5	±15	±10
Differential phase (degrees)	±3	±5	±10	±6

5.2   SOME PROPRIETARY PRODUCTS USED IN CATV AND OTHER SYSTEMS

5.2.1   Product 'Multiview', supplied by STC plc (UK)

This subsystem can be interfaced to either single-mode or graded-index multimode fiber cables. It will typically allow:

● four TV signals on one fiber
● transmission range 20 km (single-mode) or 4 km (multimode)
● minimum 50.5 dB unified weighted S/N (each channel)
● 1300 nm or 850 nm wavelengths (CW laser and APD receiver)
● 28 dB optical path loss (multi-mode version)
● surface-mounted component technology
● three PC cards per module (double-height Eurocards)
● uses 'Stratos'-type 430 optical connector
● modular construction.

Multiview is in use within several CATV networks, freeway surveillance systems and other systems for which analog video is appropriate.

5.2.2 Société Anonyme de Telecommunications (SAT) (France)

The SAT trunk fiber-optic subsystem units are available in a number of versions (some use first window, some second). They are all rack mounted, have one laser per fiber port, carry one channel to each port, have electronic control and provide a hot standby path. Other specification points include:

- maximum range 25 km
- minimum 56 dB weighted S/N
- meets a 5% differential gain and 5° differential phase requirements (as remarked in Section 5.1.3, these subsystems are designed for the French CATV networks).

A typical installed example comprises 10 second-window lasers (1300 nm) in modules built to the above specification.

As main contractor for the French networks SAT are responsible for:

- general system design
- main exchanges for video and digital telephone
- interexchange and subscriber optical transmission equipments
- cables and splices
- couplers between interactive video-image information systems and the network.

The SAT cable TV supertrunk subsystem was the only one which met the rather demanding specifications, especially regarding differential gain and phase.

5.2.3 Pirelli TR 1300-series subsystem

This is an FM/FDM subsystem with some interesting features:

- usually eight but can be up to 16 video/audio channels on one single-mode fiber (they actually *claim* a capability of up to 30 baseband audio/video signals)
- transmission range 20 km (to one location) or 12 km to two locations using an optical splitter
- 1300 nm laser transmitter, delivering – 3 dBm into fiber
- 11 dB optical path loss

- built to MIL STD 2170, giving claimed MTBF exceeding 100 000 hours
- 55.3 dB EIA weighted signal-to-noise ratio
- PIN diode photodetector at receiver.

The product is manufactured in the USA by Pirelli Advanced Communications Systems.

Some companies are currently working on video systems with capacities of 50 to 60 conventional TV channels and one example is considered next.

5.2.4   GTE Laboratories' new development

GTE have developed a subsystem that can accommodate up to 60 *conventional TV channels* or their equivalent, simultaneously on one fiber.

They use an analog technique called *sub-carrier multiplexing*. We shall not address the details here, but this technique owes a lot to television receiver processing concepts and GTE's subsystem performs the operation at microwave frequencies. Each video signal is caused to modulate a dedicated microwave carrier and the entire 'assembly' is transmitted on the fiber using a laser. TV, audio or data can be transmitted simultaneously in virtually any combination. For example the system can accommodate: 50 conventional TV channels, *plus* 4 HDTV channels *plus* 25 high quality audio or data channels.

The GTE subsystem is presently at the advanced laboratory stage but when commercially available (1990?) it will almost certainly open up new dimensions in combined services for homes and businesses.

5.3   CLOSED-CIRCUIT TELEVISION (CCTV)

CCTV applies to systems that neither produce nor receive any broadcast signals, i.e. they operate in closed 'circuits'. Examples are found in: surveillance situations (civil and military), security installations (e.g. banks, shops) and in special industrial applications (e.g. steel mills).

In any of these types of systems a relatively simple communications link must be provided between the remote video cameras and monitor/recorder units. Coaxial cable has traditionally been used in this role, but the electrical environment can often (increasingly) be such as to suggest implementation with fiber.

Video channels (usually fairly low-definition monochrome for CCTV) require a few MHz of bandwidth, but optical fibers will handle this easily. Baseband, intensity modulation is usually employed, with straightforward Manchester coding.

Fiber-based CCTV is in fact desirable for a number of reasons, including:

- There exists immunity to all forms of electromagnetic interference (EMI) and high-quality monochrome pictures are received (interference is a well-known problem in metallic-cable CCTV systems).
- This also implies that no special cable routing is required and there is no need to avoid proximity to electrical machinery or other sources of interference.
- Also, no EMI or RFI is generated by the optical-fiber cabling; making it immune to tapping (unless physically interrupted, which is detectable by the user) and inherently secure.

Typical CCTV links of these types cover ranges up to 2 km using 50/125 or 62.5/125 cables and they are suited to either permanent or portable installations. Several companies worldwide offer such complete links.

5.4 FINANCIAL SERVICES SYSTEMS

The continuing expansion of trading-room facilities in major world cities represents a further significant application area for fiber-optic systems. The problems posed in planning these types of systems include the existence of and need for:

- Relatively large numbers of users operating in close proximity (typically hundreds in one building).
- High resolution color video switched facilities.
- All switching and interconnection operations to take place in a separate communications room.
- Provision for interfaces such as RS 232C, IBM X.21 and RS 422.
- External connections made available through telephone lines, satellite communications terminals and microwave radio.

Fiber optics are well suited to an environment such as this.

One example of such a system is in place at the Broadgate development in the City of London. The financial institution operating at this location required a facility for commodity and money market trading by just over eight hundred dealer positions distributed throughout the five storeys of the building. Electrical coaxial cabling and shielded data wires were at first considered as a possible approach, but the total space required for this would have required one meter increases in all floor heights and hence an increase in the total height of the building and this was clearly unacceptable. Cabling generally also makes a significant contribution to the total structural weight loading of a building and electrical cable has a greater impact than optical fiber in this respect.

An optical fiber system using an advanced form of star topology was ultimately chosen and was brought into operation in late summer 1987. With this data network each dealer is connected using one 12 mm diameter fiber cable and the thickness of the suspended flooring is only 400 mm. A total length of 128 mm of fiber-optic cable was installed more cheaply and easily than would have been the case with electrical cables.

Several installations of fiber-optic systems have also been completed in the USA, mainland Europe and Japan.

The largest in the world is located in the World Financial Center in New York and is operated by Shearson Lehmann Brothers, the securities dealers. It comprises about 5000 km of fiber, over 60 000 fiber-optic connectors, 12 700 transmit/receive video modules and about 5000 data modules. The decision to use fiber was determined by the following factors:

(i)   Low attenuation.
(ii)   Freedom from cross-talk.
(iii) Immunity from EMI.

In all these respects metallic cable would not have met the requirements.

Doubtless these successful examples of fiber penetration will pave the way for many future systems.

5.5   MILITARY AND AEROSPACE APPLICATIONS

Fiber-optic technology is increasingly penetrating military and aerospace applications, most strongly in the USA but also increasingly in Western Europe.

Typical military applications include: strategic and tactical communications systems, guided weapons, antisubmarine warfare nets, nuclear testing, fixed plant installations. Aerospace applications, civil and military, embrace avionics data bases and spacecraft systems. Secure data links are also of interest to both civil (e.g. police) and military users.

As with other areas of high technology much so-called military fiber-optic activity is a development of currently available commercial products with appropriate adaptation to meet military specifications. Ease and speed of operation and ruggedness are especially significant here.

The basic advantages generally accepted for fiber optics also apply in these applications, with low weight of cable being important for guided weapons, avionics and spacecraft. For secure communications the immunity of fiber-optic cable to electrical interference and the difficulties of tapping are both of considerable importance. A relatively new technique is being developed to detect tapping and this involves the application of a thin coating of conductive material covering the fiber. Any damage, accidental or otherwise occurring to this coating, can easily be (electrically) detected and located and action can then be promulgated to stop the unauthorized tapping. The coating itself must not degrade significantly over time; protected aluminum being the preferred choice.

For the past ten years and more government defense departments have placed a high level of priority to procuring military electronic systems that are hardened against malfunction due to nuclear electromagnetic pulse (NEMP) and nuclear radiation. The use of optical fiber for transmission can clearly be critical here. For example, US production ground-launched cruise missiles (GLCMs) have employed fiber-optic systems.

In military applications the optical fibers to be chosen must themselves be highly resistant to the light-attenuating effects of nuclear radiation and only certain types of fibers can operate at both the shorter (850 nm) and the longer (1300 nm) wavelengths in this hostile radiation environment. High OH fluorosilicate clad fibers provide excellent radiation resistance at the shorter wavelengths but their intrinsic losses rise substantially and thus inhibit operation at the longer wavelengths. Germanium-doped fibers exhibit improved performance at the longer wavelengths for fiber-optic transmission but are not resistant to nuclear radiation at the shorter wavelengths. The low OH borofluorosilicate clad fibers such as those manufactured by Dainichi of Japan are the only types that provide good radiation resistance across the wavelength range. Reliable standards-based test procedures for these fibers are under consideration by NATO and the US Department of Defense.

As a successor to the Tornado era the four-nation European Fighter Aircraft (EFA) is planned for service in the mid-1990s.

The proposed optical data bus for the EFA will be based on the developing NATA standard 3910, being a high speed serial bus controlled by a relatively low speed MIL STD 1553 bus designed to specification STANAG 3838. The bit rate is 20 Mbit/s for the 3910 standard, line coding is into Manchester II format and there is 32-way physical addressing.

6

Local and metropolitan area networks (LANs and MANs)

In this chapter we shall examine LANs, MANs, backbone and mainframe links for data networks.

6.1 POWER BUDGETS

The concept of a power budget is outlined in simple terms in Chapter 1.

The principal aim is to find the maximum practical range of any fiber-optic link. This range depends critically on the type of transmitter, LED or laser, and on the type of fiber, amongst other factors. An assessment is made of all the power levels and losses along the link and an indication of features that must be considered is given in Fig. 6.1.

Coupling losses occur from the transmitter to the fiber (1) (launching loss), we then have fiber loss itself (2), splice loss (3) (a splice is a permanently fused connection between fibers) and connector loss (4). In many practical systems there are other losses such as those attributable to multi-port couplers, etc.

The total transmission loss between launchers is then the sum of total fiber loss and splice plus connector losses. For example, the fiber might

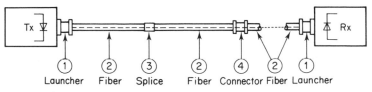

Fig. 6.1 Power losses along a typical fiber link (the 'launchers' are connector ports).

lose 2.625 dB/kilometer and each of three connectors might lose 0.8 dB. The figure of 2.625 dB is chosen to keep the arithmetic simple and yet representative here. If we have 8 km of fiber (total, sum of lengths) then the total transmission loss L_T (dB) is:

$$L_T = (2.625 \times 8) + (0.3 \times 2) + (0.8 \times 3) = 21 + 0.6 + 2.4$$
$$= 24 \text{ dB}$$

This is equivalent to pretending that we had 8 km of fiber with a loss per km of

$$24 \text{ dB}/8 \text{ km} = 3 \text{ dB/km}$$

Based upon this representative calculation, link designs can be compared in terms of power budgets — initially for medium-range links using fairly high-quality fibers as shown in Fig. 6.2. This situation could, for example, apply to links within a metropolitan area network (MAN).

The numerical notation on the curves represents:

(1) Optical source power.
(2) Optical power coupled into the fiber.
(3) Optical power at output end of the fiber.
(4) Optical power at detector.
(5) Minimum required receiver power (including a margin to ensure continuous operation to specification).

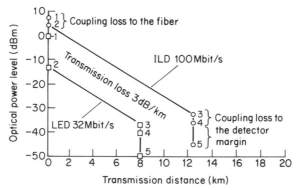

Fig. 6.2 Typical power budgets for fiber links with laser (ILD) and LED as alternative transmitting sources (with grateful acknowledgment to Y. Suematsu and K.-I. Iga from whose work *Introduction to Optical Fiber Communications* this figure was taken with their permission).

Notice that, to start with the LED produces less power than the laser (1 mW against 5 mW). This is actually not particularly conservative since many LEDs achieve much less than 1 mW and several lasers can provide 50 mW or even 100 mW. But the choice here serves to make the desired point.

Also, and very significantly, the coupling losses to the fiber (launching) differ greatly according to the type of transmitter, in this situation about 12 dB for LED-to-fiber, but only about 2 dB for laser-to-fiber, i.e. considerably reduced in this situation.

In both cases the maximum BER at the receiver is 10^{-9}, being a typical maximum for data networks.

We can summarize the contrasts here by pointing out that the LED-based system can extend to 8 km maximum range at 32 Mbit/s, whereas the *laser-based system* will cover 12.5 km maximum range but also at the much higher data rate of 100 Mbit/s.

LANs generally involve shorter-range links, often extending to only a few kilometers, but relatively low-quality fibers are frequently used. The power-budget diagram that now follows (Fig. 6.3) applies to a LED-driven multimode fiber cable with a loss of 10 dB/km.

For ranges up to 2 km the received optical power remains at a tolerable level for practical systems, always exceeding about − 48 dBm. However, a range of 5 km would necessitate a very sensitive receiver involving critical design and attracting a much higher unit price.

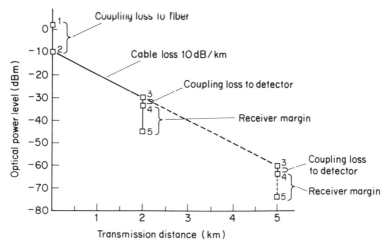

Fig. 6.3 Power budgets applicable to typical LAN links.

These comments apply where such links are operated at low to moderate bit rates, e.g. Kbit/s to several Mbit/s, i.e. for 'first generation' and some 'second generation' LANs. We shall examine these 'generations' in more detail shortly.

6.2 BACKBONE AND MAINFRAME DATA LINKS

6.2.1 Aspects of basic commercially available links

In these links the line coding must be organized in a fashion suited to the nature of the optical-fiber link. Typical codes involve 'non-return to zero' (NRZ), Manchester, Cambridge ring or other coding such as HDB3. Most of these codes are dealt with in detail in Chapter 4.

Fairly simple data communications systems are available off-the-shelf from companies like Plessey, RCA, Hewlett-Packard, etc. They are mostly 'TTL compatible', i.e. they operate on 0 V to $+5$ V nominal power supply levels and will typically provide bit rates up to 20 Mbit/s (20 M baud), ranges to just over 1 km, a maximum BER of 10^{-9} and an allowable total maximum loss through the link of 20 dB.

Optical fibers in mainframe computer communications

As an example of a specific case we shall consider ICL's (UK) 'Macrolan'. In 1985 ICL announced its new Series 39 mainframe computers. A nodal architecture has been developed which allows Series 39 processing units ('nodes') and high-speed peripheral devices to be linked together in modular fashion, without complex controllers, such that it can operate at maximum efficiency. This is made possible through the implementation of a high-speed (50 Mbit/s) local area network called Macrolan which employs optical fiber cabling to transmit data between nodes and peripheral units having separations extending to 1.5 km.

The cables are 5 mm in diameter and their implementation has significantly reduced the overall cabling requirements, hence decreasing costs, increasing reliability and improving systems flexibility. Each 5 mm cable contains two optical fibers, one for transmission and one for reception.

Nodes or peripherals are linked to the cable by means of a Macrolan Port Switch Unit which is smaller than an average briefcase and will fit on to a wall. Each Port Switch has six transceiver ports connected using internal couplers and further units may be cascaded to provide up to 15 stations on a single Macrolan.

Failure in an individual station (node or peripheral) will not affect the operation itself since the Port Switch Unit will sense such a failure and will bridge the gap to bypass the faulty unit.

The use of fiber optics in this type of role is expected to generally increase, given effective commercial examples such as the ICL system.

6.3 LOCALIZED COMPUTER NETWORKS

In this section we study a specific example (a mixed-media network — not a proprietary product).

A specific practical example of a computer network employing a mixture of cable types is shown in Fig. 6.4. In each of the office areas and in the library unit two or three computer terminals are installed.

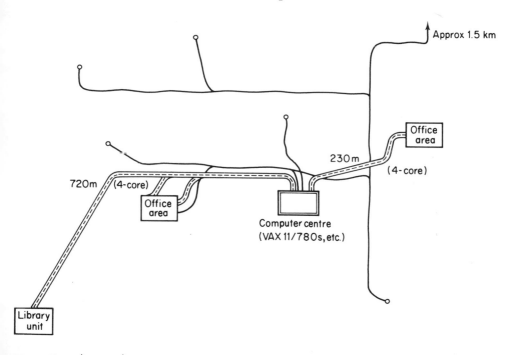

===== Focom 'COMSIL' step-index PCS optical fibers

⊃— Metallic cables (some copper multipair, some triaxial)

Fig. 6.4 Example of a multiplexed network comprising a mixture of fiber and metallic cables.

Notice that the full distance between the furthest office area and library is under 1 km. This network incorporates a multiplexing interface unit which can handle up to 32 duplex channels. Data streams, to and from terminals, etc, are at 9600 bit/s and the multiplexer ensures the assembly of these to form a 7 Mbit/s serial stream over the fibers. For the (relatively short) distances here the fairly inexpensive PCS step-index fibers are used.

A number of the links are implemented with metal cables, coaxial or multi-core. Where optical fibers are used their choice in this case was originally dictated by: low cost of handling and laying (especially within ducts also used for electrical power cables), immunity to interference caused by adjacent electrical cables and by lightning strikes, and future expandability/up-grading of the system. This system has been operating since early 1984 with only minor problems.

More comprehensive details regarding some local area networks (LANs) are now given in the next section.

6.4 LOCAL AREA NETWORKS (LANs): EXAMPLES

6.4.1 Definitions and suppliers

A LAN may be very simply defined as a controlled set of interconnections between a number of computer terminals, microcomputers and other data facilities, spread around a local or 'limited' area. The *aim* of a LAN has been defined as 'the provision of a versatile and dependable transmission path around a group of users'.

The basis for the standardization of LANs is through the International Standards Organization (ISO) who have produced a reference model for Open Systems Interconnection (OSI). In particular, the model involves conceptual layers as shown in Fig. 6.5.

Here we are primarily concerned with the physical medium (optical fiber cable in this case) the physical layer and the required electro-optic interfaces.

It is useful to think in terms of three generations of LANs; defined according to bit-rate capabilities, provision of facilities and state of development:

● *First-generation LANs:* Up to about 10 Mbit/s. Communicating between elements of the electronic office (e.g. word processors), or in distributed computer systems. Commercially available.

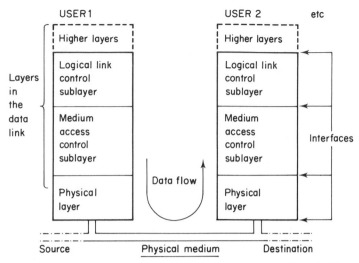

Fig. 6.5 The Open Systems Interconnection (OSI) standard model for LANs.

- *Second-generation LANs:* Up to around 100 Mbit/s. To be capable of handling a useful number of telephone terminals, in addition to first-generation LAN communications (considerably demanding technology). Some commercially available.
- *Third-generation LANs:* Around and above 1000 Mbit/s (1 Gbit/s). Very-high-speed interactive computing. Inclusive of real-time video signals. Under active development.

Optical fiber systems are now substantially impacting first and second-generation LANs, bringing the advantages outlined in Chapter 1. Bandwidth, and therefore ultimately bit-rate capabilities, are likely always to be limited by the electro-optic interfaces (and not by possibilities afforded by the fiber cables themselves, certainly when single-mode is implemented).

Other advantages of using fiber include the major aspects previously dealt with:

- high level of information security
- high integrity in EMI-prone environments
- future expandability: again, particularly where single-mode can be justified.

Some market studies indicate a dominance of LANs using optical fibers by the early 1990s: at least the increasing penetration of this medium into these types of networks appears to be assured.

At present fiber LANs do suffer the restriction of a relatively low maximum number of nodes (depending upon topological options) and the unit prices still tend to exceed conventional metallic cable/electronic systems. But these fiber-optic unit prices are falling.

In general, LANs may be 'broadband' or 'baseband'. Current fiber-optic LANs operate in baseband, i.e. information is modulated directly on to the transmitting device and is carried by the fibers as a serial data stream using Manchester code, HDB3, etc, as previously described.

Table 6.1 A selection of fiber-optic LANs

LAN name	Type
Codenet	Ethernet compatible
Datapipe	275 Mbit/s fiber optic (mainframes)
Dataring +	Cambridge ring
FDDI	Fiber optic, FDDI standard
WhisperLAN	Fiber optic (from FiberCom)
F-128	Fiber optic (dual, 22.88 Mbit/s)
Hi Net	Loop. IBM compatible
Isolan	IEEE 802.3 (10 Mbit/s standard, fiber optic)
KFO 7000	Fiber optics, based on Cambridge ring
LAN2	Tokenbus IEEE 802.4
LANDLINK 50	50 Mbit/s link
MAP network	Specification 3.0. 150 nodes
Macrolan	Fiber optic (50 Mbit/s)
Melnet	Duplex ring
Net/One	Shared logic
Netware/S-Net	Star-configured file server
NET-ONE	Fiber optic
Pirelli-Focom 1800 and 2000 series	Fiber optics
Pronet	Process control
Plant	Cambridge ring
Pacxnet	Office automation
Symbnet	Tree and branch
Tensornet	LAN for tensor micros
Transring 3000	Cambridge ring

6.4.2 Network topologies

For any desired network using any proposed transmission medium, there are four general possible topological layouts and these are indicated in simple form in Fig. 6.6.

Variations on topologies (a), (b) and (c) are often used in fiber-optic LANs and (c), the tree topology, is frequently used in CATV and related networks.

In practical systems the terminals are generally referred to as nodes

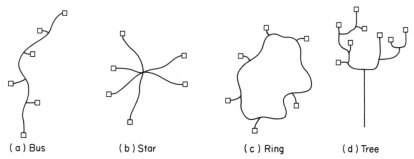

(a) Bus   (b) Star   (c) Ring   (d) Tree

Fig. 6.6 Four general network topologies.

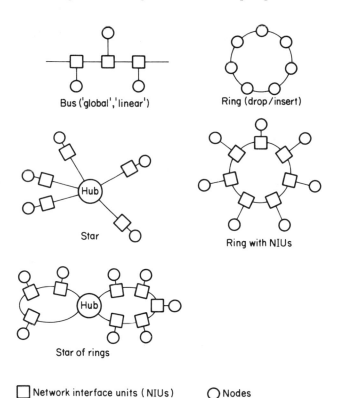

Bus ('global','linear')   Ring (drop/insert)

Star   Ring with NIUs

Star of rings

☐ Network interface units (NIUs)   ○ Nodes

Fig. 6.7 Network topologies that are potentially suitable for fiber system implementation.

and network interface units (NIUs) are required to connect into the network in most cases.

Thus, in rather more detail, topologies suited to fiber-optic implementation appear as shown in Fig. 6.7.

In the case of star-configured fiber-optic LANs the hub is often made active, as shown in Fig. 6.8.

Transmitters and receivers are abbreviated Tx and Rx respectively here: in practice each node will require its own transmitter *and* receiver. The electronic circuits within the hub essentially play the role of a traditional PBX or packet switch and can process simultaneous inputs without collisions (conversion, regeneration, access control and switching is performed here). This type of configuration avoids the use of passive star couplers.

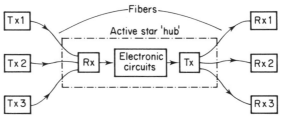

Fig. 6.8 Basic configuration of an active star network.

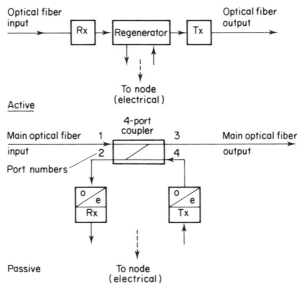

Fig. 6.9 Active and passive network interface units (NIUs).

Network Interface Units or Modules (NIUs or NIMs) may in general be 'active' or 'passive', as shown in Fig. 6.9.

The active NIU saves having a 4-port coupler but a failure in the receiver, transmitter or regenerator puts a break in the network.

Fiber-optic *ring LAN* topologies are next considered in rather more detail since these are often implemented. As can be seen from Fig. 6.10 both active and passive versions are possible.

In the active ring interfacing and regeneration takes place at each node location whereas in the passive version 4-port couplers are required making the ring itself all-optical. The comments given above for active or passive NIUs apply here. A problem with the passive ring

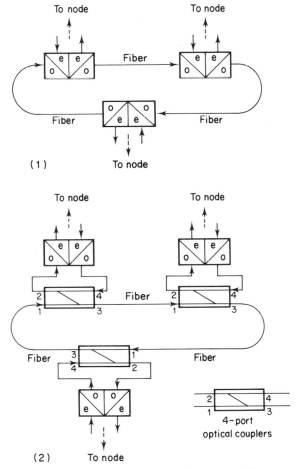

Fig. 6.10   Active (1) and passive (2) fiber ring LAN topologies.

is that signal echo can then occur, there being two possible optical paths between NIUs.

An NIU can be designed with fail-safe attributes and this is shown in Fig. 6.11.

In the event of NIU failure the optical switch is automatically tripped ON and the signals then by-pass the main unit via ports '2' of the couplers. Internal optical route reversal ('loop-back') is activated if main fibers or connections happen to break. In all cases of any failure network maintenance warnings are automatically triggered. Ericsson is, for example, currently offering such a switch.

Star LANs are also available and the general active star has already

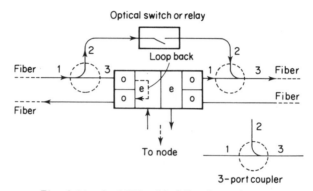

Fig. 6.11 An NIU with fail-safe attributes.

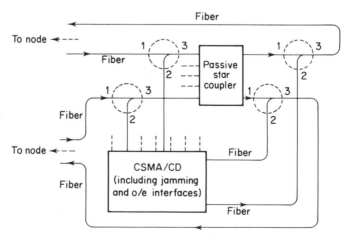

Fig. 6.12 Passive star LAN with centralized CSMA/CD (see text for explanation of these abbreviations).

been described. Some organizations produce passive star LANs and these can incorporate centralized collision detection and jamming facilities (CSMA/CD) (see next sub-section). The basic configuration is shown in Fig. 6.12 which indicates two connections to nodes which require NIUs; in practice there can be up to several hundred nodes.

6.4.3 Access methods

There are a number of methods used as access protocols in LANs, major techniques being: token passing, CSMA/CD and TDMA.

Token passing can be used with ring or bus topologies. It is an access protocol that permits a terminal to transmit only on receipt of a special circulating bit sequence.

CSMA/CD (carrier sense multiple access, with collision detection) is used with bus and some star topologies. It operates by contention, each terminal competes for access to the bus. A terminal wishing to transmit attempts this when the bus is quiet. Simultaneously, received signals are monitored by this terminal to check for corruption resulting from collision with another transmission present at the same time. In the event of such a collision its effect at this terminal is 'enforced' with the use of a jamming signal and all current transmissions are stopped.

Repeated retransmission attempts are made, with designed-in delays to reduce the probability of further collisions, until successful transmission occurs. When carrying rather long data packets over short cables, and with offered traffic about 20% or less of maximum, the system works extremely well.

TDMA (time-division multiple access) was originally devised for digital microwave and satellite communications systems. It is still used with many such systems as well as with some fiber-optic systems. Fixed time-slots are made available, regardless of whether they are actually used. The complete end-to-end bit sequences within each time slot are usually called a *serial packet*, each of which comprises: source and destination addresses, data bits, control and status bits.

The system is accessed through terminal stations and repeaters. Transmission is into an empty packet or packets and reception occurs via packet address recognition. A monitor station monitors the integrity of the system during normal operation and places framing bits around packets in the initializing process.

6.4.4   Other mixed-media LANs

A number of LANs employ metallic cables (coaxial or twisted-pair) in some links and optical fibers in others to take appropriate advantages of each medium. Amongst these are some versions of Cambridge ring LANs and the 'Apollo Domain' systems.

The Cambridge ring LAN system operates at the same data rate as Ethernet (i.e. 10 Mbit/s) but differs radically in its topology. One or more serial packets of data circulate within the closed loop, which physically covers the area to be served by the network. The access method used is TDMA.

In their electrical form Cambridge ring LANs use their own data codes known as Cambridge ring codes. In one such code each downward pulse transition means that a data transition from 1 to 0 is about to follow and the code rate is maintained the same as the original information rate. Codes — modulation formats — are explained in Chapter 4.

To convert to an optical fiber system each two-wire line in a Cambridge ring may simply be replaced by an optical fiber and optical transmitters and receivers installed. But there are two significant drawbacks to this simple approach:

(i)   Only a small bandwidth is required and it is therefore wasteful to use two fibers.

(ii) Manufacturing variations result in different propagating delays in fibers having the same physical lengths. This produces de-synchronization between data transitions on the two paths, causing bit errors.

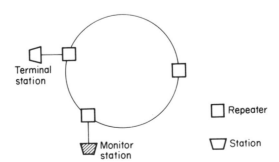

Fig. 6.13   Basic schematic diagram of the Cambridge ring LAN concept.

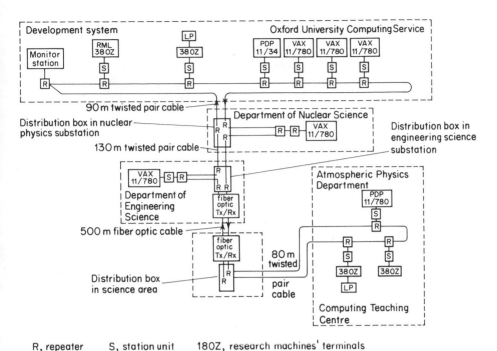

R, repeater   S, station unit   180Z, research machines' terminals
RML, 380Z microcomputer system

Fig. 6.14 Architecture of the Cambridge ring LAN installed at Oxford University.

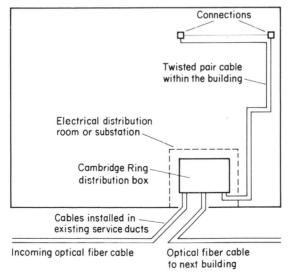

Fig. 6.15 Standard connections for Cambridge ring LANs.

Manchester code effectively eliminates these problems and clock recovery is relatively easy at the receiver. Although the bandwidth requirement is now much greater, being twice the data rate, increasing the bandwidth does not present a problem with optical fibers. (It can, however, present problems with electronics and the optoelectronic interfaces.)

A good example of a Cambridge ring LAN exists around the Science Area at Oxford University. This was manufactured and installed by GEC plc, uses 4 km of 160/200 micron step-index fiber cables and enables the inner operation of a number of differing types of computers and peripherals. Such terminals include: DEC VAX 11/780s, Research Machines RM 380 Z6s line printers and disc drive units. Systems layouts are shown in Figs 6.14 and 6.15.

In early 1985 'Apollo Domain' LAN and terminal equipment worth over \$0.6m was ordered by three UK universities. Bradford University, for example, has installed such a LAN for CAD work, supporting eight workstations in its four engineering departments. Distances involved are up to 2 km and departments are linked via the university computing center. Optical fibers, used for some of the links, minimize the effects of electrical interference. The other universities installing these LANs are Imperial College and Liverpool.

6.4.5   Problems imposed by fiber couplers

Cumulative losses due to fiber couplers are much larger than for their coaxial cable counterparts. A unidirectional bus containing 20 passive fiber couplers will suffer at least 60 dB of attenuation between extreme ports.

Because of this, a direct fiber substitution in a *bussed LAN* would restrict the system to typically only 8 couplers — 8 users. The Ethernet LAN can have up to 100 couplers in 500 m of cable.

Also, at present, multimode fiber couplers cost approximately US \$100 each with at least three connectors required per coupler (four for a 4-port) at about \$20 each. Thus, 8 couplers plus connectors cost approximately \$1300 to \$1400 on this basis. Re-connection, i.e. mount/de-mount difficulties can also be experienced with such couplers. For the above reasons *active NIUs* are often employed in fiber-optic systems.

6.4.6 Other proprietary fiber-optic LANs

Ethernet LANs (see Fig. 6.16) were originally developed by the Xerox Corporation; considerable support has also come from computer companies such as DEC and ICL.

A number of companies supply Ethernet compatible fiber-optic local area networks, amongst them the Codenoll Technology Corporation. These bus-topology LANs operate at 10 Mbit/s and use the wavelengths 830 or 1300 nm. Codenoll also supply *links* that operate at data rates as high as 50 Mbit/s (with LEDs and TTL logic) and 150 Mbit/s (with lasers and ECL logic). Star configurations can be formed from basic buses.

A comparison of many current LANs using fiber optics reveal that:

(i)   Most ranges (spans) are less than 2 km with the largest often about 9 km
(ii)   Most use LED transmitters and PIN receivers.
(iii) Several use Manchester coding.
(iv)   The maximum number of nodes varies from 16 to 65 536.
(v)   Bit rates range from 3.4 to 100 Mbit/s, with step-index fibers often used at lower rates and graded-index (GI) at the higher rates.

Bit-error rates are required to be lower than 10^{-9} in all cases.

All the access methods used have already been described with the exceptions of 'hub access' (Hubnet — described presently) and 'locomotive' in connection with TRW's D-Net.

In the D-Net a specialized node called the 'locomotive generator' produces pulsed sequences that define the access time slots for the network interfaces. These time slots are usually termed 'windows'. This results in a relatively high degree of network utilization as a function of time and therefore, unlike many of the other networks, bit rates in the

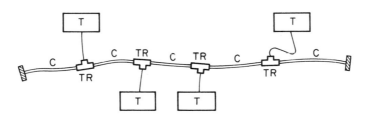

T, Terminal   TR, Transceiver (plus coupler)   C, Coaxial cable bus

Fig. 6.16 Ethernet LAN layout using conventional electrical coaxial cable.

region of hundreds of Mbit/s are feasible. Because network delay is tightly controlled, packetized voice transmission is also accommodated.

Ethernet-style LANs have a number of shortcomings; in particular:

(a) Degraded performance under heavy traffic loads.
(b) Low efficiency at high bit rates.
(c) The serious problem of optical coupler losses in fiber-optic versions

In an effort to overcome these disadvantages the CANSTAR Corporation (of Canada) in collaboration with the University of Toronto's Computer Systems Research Group have developed a novel type of LAN known as Hubnet. This LAN no longer has any 'bus' or similar linking arrangement but, instead, possesses a relatively sophisticated star hub containing signal selection and broadcasting facilities. It may be assumed that, on start-up for example, there are initially no signals at the hub and then a number of signals arrive simultaneously. Under these conditions one signal is selected arbitrarily and all others are blocked until the hub is clear and ready to process another signal ('hub access').

The Hubnet system may be cascaded to form more complex LANs, enabling up to 65 536 nodes to be accommodated.

Fibernet 2 (Fig. 6.17), an optical-fiber version of Ethernet, is realized with a *completely different topology* in order to largely overcome the drawbacks of direct substitution. Like Ethernet, it still operates at 10 Mbit/s and uses Manchester coding. But in Fibernet 2 the transceiver associated with each terminal or station is connected to a central 'Hub' by a duplex fiber cable (two fibers in one cable).

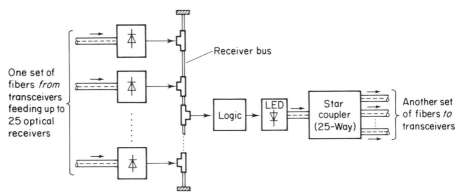

Fig. 6.17   General arrangement of the Fibernet 2 LAN system.

The output data stream from each terminal goes to an *optical receiver* (there are up to 25 of these). At the *electrical* outputs from the optical receivers the signals couple into a conventional, *highly localized*, receiver bus which feeds logic driving a transmitter LED. This internal electrical bus can be visualized as a kind of 'mini-Ethernet'. (In the event of a collision, it is detected on this receiver bus and a jamming sequence ensues; as explained for Ethernet.)

Optical signals from the LED are input to a 25-way *star coupler* which efficiently distributes optical power to the receivers of the transceivers. Output signal levels are typically 14 dB down on the input.

If instead of this system we had directly implemented a *unidirectional bus with 25 passive couplers* in series a total loss of more than *75 dB* between extreme ports would have resulted. This would exceed by far the operable power budget and such a system would be unworkable. The Xerox Corporation offer the Fibernet 2 LAN.

6.4.7 Braided rings and double rings (Fig. 6.18)

Reliability can become a problem with rings particularly since just one cable break or one repeater failure disables the entire network (although special auto-reconfiguring approaches can alleviate this).

There exist more reliable architectures than the simple ring, in particular the braided ring and double ring. These are becoming important as second-generation LANs enter service, with their higher

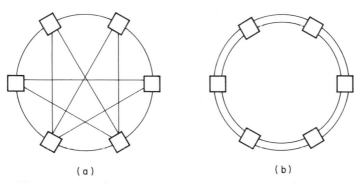

(a)   (b)

Fig. 6.18 Braided (a) and double (b) ring LAN architectures.

data rates. Schematic diagrams indicating the general architectures of braided and double-ring LANs are provided in Fig. 6.18.

Racal-Milgo, for example, offer their 'Planet' LAN with a double-ring optical-fiber option.

6.4.8 Fiber-optic LAN standards

Standards applicable to fiber-optic LANs are in active preparation by a number of bodies with strong commercial representation. There are two notable North American organizations: the IEEE (Institute for Electrical and Electronic Engineers) and ANSI (American National Standards Institute).

The IEEE has been concerned with standards for systems operating at rates up to 10 Mbit/s. In particular, the IEEE 802.5 token-passing protocol standard exists. This is currently applied to 8 Mbit/s serial transmission but it is anticipated that it will be up-graded to 16 Mbit/s by 1990.

ANSI have been presenting in detail specifications for LANs operating at data rates up to 100 Mbit/s using optical fiber (and mixed media).

The X3T9.5 committee of ANSI currently specify a Fiber Distributed Data Interface (FDDI) which comprises a token-passing ring operating at 100 Mbit/s and allowing various options to suit different companies' planned products.

The FDDI is actually a double ring since it combines two independent counter-rotating rings.

Other aspects of the FDDI specification include:

● Support for up to 1000 nodes;
● A maximum distance of 2 km between nodes;
● Up to 200 km of total circumference;
● Use of 62.5/125 or 85/125 fiber operating at 850 nm;
● Use of a special coding scheme known as 4B/5B.

The 4B/5B code is described in Chapter 4 where it is pointed out that the modulation rate is reduced to only about 60% of that required for Manchester.

The consequences include reduced costs, simplified design and eased installation. The pulses are transmitted optically using the NRZ-L format.

There are two kinds of terminal station in FDDI: Class A and Class B. Class A stations connect both rings simultaneously whereas with Class B only one ring is connected, the purpose being to optimize design and reduce costs. There are also wiring concentrators which are provided at hub nodes so that several stations may be connected at such locations when desired.

A second-generation FDDI LAN standard is now in preparation.

6.4.9 Fiber-optic cable installation

In some respects optical fiber cables provide advantages when compared to metallic cable installation, due mainly to the relatively low weight and freedom from electrical interference with this medium. The low weight means that reel-handling is easier and the freedom from electrical interference allows cables (power or communications) to be installed in close proximity to each other. In all cases, however, careful attention must be paid to minimum bending radii, details of which should be obtained prior to installation.

Some rules-of-thumb regarding minimum bending radii for *fibers* were provided in Chapter 2. As reasonable guidance for *cable* (indoor) a minimum of approximately ten times the outside diameter of the cable should be allowed. Thus, a 7-mm cable should not be bent through a radius smaller than about 70 mm.

It is essential to distinguish between intra-building (i.e. within a building) and inter-building installations. Within an organization's premises the environment may be relatively benign and fairly lightly-jacketed cables can be used.

Optical fiber cables run to each floor of a building where they are demultiplexed ('MUX') and connected to one side of a cross-connect facility. User terminals are attached to the other (electrical) side of the cross-connect facility and are bridged to the 'MUX' terminations. The 'MUX' is acting essentially as an NIU. A new user is simply connected to one of the spare channels and upon disconnection from the cross-connect socket, a user's previously busy channel just becomes a spare.

6.4.10 LAN and MAN installation techniques

LANs

A number of optical fiber cable installation techniques have been developed on an operationally acceptable status.

Compared with metallic cables fiber cables may:

(1) More easily be pulled (or 'blown', see presently) into ducts — taking advantage of their relatively low weight. Also they can be handled in longer lengths (with fewer joints) due to low losses.
(2) Use existing ducting, etc, more efficiently (install more cables) due to small diameters.
(3) Use existing or new high-voltage open-wire electricity power lines as a support structure (which takes advantage of immunity from EMI).

For pulling, ends of optical fiber cables have been bent around so as to hand-form an eye. Where space is available in the ducting special pulling heads have been used.

For lengths typically 3 km or more specialized cable-roller guides and intermediate take-up units are available.

One technique consists of:

(a) inexpensive, easily-handled plastic tubing pulled into existing ducts or installed within a building structure, followed by;
(b) fiber cables blown through using compressed air (avoids any possibly damaging strain, or at least performance-degrading bends/kinks).

There is also a substantial reduction in installation costs as a result of this approach — very important since installation costs so often predominate.

Firms such as Siemens of West Germany and British Telecom have used this technique. New developments are also being announced in this (e.g. Optical Fibers/Architron).

MANs

Outdoors, cables may be laid in new runs (this is usually an expensive approach) or, where wayleaves are obtainable, along railway tracks (e.g. Mercury Communication UK). Another possible wayleave is the high-voltage power line approach referred to under LANs and the Siemens Company, for example, have installed cables using this wayleave.

Raychem (with headquarters in Menlo Park, California) have developed a helical wrapping method for installing fiber-optic cables along power lines. The helical approach was chosen for aerodynamic reasons and the wrapping machine is attached to the overhead conductor, then towed from ground level. Achievements and features of this technique include:

(i)   One cable can be installed per day by established overhead line teams (no further training).
(ii) The cable has a 'high-voltage non-tracking oversheath'.
(iii) About two to four graded index telecommunications fibers are incorporated in each cable.
(iv) Easy alignment low-loss jointing is enabled.

This installation technique has been applied in Norway, the UK and in New Zealand, with satisfactory results on power lines with voltages up to 132 kV. The Norwegian installations have verified that the use of the helically wrapped optical cable does not contribute significantly to snow loading of the overhead lines.

7

Long-distance trunk telecommunications

7.1 INTRODUCTION

By 'long-distance' in this context we mean distances beyond those generally associated with LANs, MANs or more private WANs, i.e. total loop distances in the tens, hundreds or thousands of kilometers regions. Nationally and internationally we therefore include the so-called Public Switched Neworks (PSNs).

Nationally, a PSN is the telephone and data network installed and operated by the PTT (Posts, Telephones and Telegraphs) in a particular country and made available to household and business subscribers at large on a rent/lease/charge-per-call basis. The networks usually have a star configuration with switching facilities at the nodes (switching exchanges) and may in general employ a mix of microwave, metallic cable and fiber-optic links.

In many countries and regions of the world extensive fiber-optic trunk networks are now in place, handling increased traffic and with spare capacity available. This has led to a continuing relatively saturated market in this sector. For example, in the USA NTT and Bell have substantial national networks, in Japan a wide PSN is in place and in the UK both British Telecom and Mercury Communications have installed a great deal of fiber into their systems.

The prospect of the Integrated Services Digital Network (ISDN) is gaining impetus worldwide, with extensive digitization of telecommunication systems.

Internationally, long-distance trunk telecommunications now require implementation by *consortia*; no single company, however large, can handle such large-scale projects.

7.2 NATIONAL TRUNK SYSTEMS

In general PSNs within a country or a region operate at three distinct levels as follows:

Trunks. These link major switching centers throughout a particular country serving areas with typically some tens or hundreds of thousands of subscribers and acting as gateways for international communications. Fiber-optic trunks often work at 8, 34, and 140 Mbit/s and, on the shorter high density routes in PSNs, at 565 Mbit/s. Single-mode fibers and laser transmitter/PIN-FET receive links are preferred for the higher speed and/or longer links but multimode/LED links have been installed in other situations. Repeater spacing with single-mode fiber averages about 30 km with the average distance between switching centers about 50 km.

The junction network. This is the interconnection network between a switching center and its 15 to 20 local exchanges, each of which serves a sub-group of between 100 (in some rural areas) to 10 000 or so subscribers. The junction network also includes links between local exchanges in busy areas, some of which may be served by different switching centers. At this level of the PSN multimode fiber-optic links operate at 8 Mbit/s on two fiber cables of typical length 10 km. Signal regeneration is not usually required here.

The local communications network. This distributes signals to household subscribers (and PABXs) from the local exchanges and represents by far the greatest concentration of links and equipment in the PSN. To date there are very few fiber-optic subscriber links, outside of some pilot schemes, and the first penetration is likely to be through the provision of ISDN services to the business community in which case transmission will be 64 Kbit/s or above on 2-fiber cables of average 'loop' length 1.0 km. The fibers *may* be multimode but this is by no means certain. In fact, interest in both the USA and the UK at least is tending to move towards single-mode even in this application.

There can be no doubt that the '*local loop*' penetration will be a major new market sector for fiber optics when it arrives. It will effectively operate at business and domestic consumer level and will therefore be much more sensitive to unit prices than other fiber-optic systems implemented thus far.

Although the local loop is likely to become so significant (probably early 1990s in USA and mid-1990s elsewhere), it is beyond the specific scope of long-distance trunk in telecommunications.

Some European countries have notable communications up-grading or related prospects/potential. In Spain a $30 million joint venture project between Corning Glass and Compania Telefonica Nacional de Espana will produce 85 000 km of fiber per year started in mid-1988 with production rising to 110 000 km per year in 1995. This fiber will be used in Spain's national telecommunications improvement program. The telecommunications authorities of Portugal and Yugoslavia have announced major overhaul plans for their networks. Portugal's program is referred to as a 'long-term' project worth around $850 million in total with ITT supplying digital exchanges initially, valued at about $70 million. The Yugoslavian up-grade amounts to a $1 billion modernization and expansion of its international and domestic telecommunications network to be completed over the time-scale 1987 to 1990. The specific fiber-optic content is not know for these projects but it is certain to be substantial.

A consortium comprising ANT of West Germany, GEC of the UK, SAT of France and Telettra of Italy have recently agreed to spend about $30 million developing an optical fiber broadband transmission system and the project has the backing of the EC's 'Eureka' program. The system will use two single-mode fibers. Completion of the demonstration system for the long distance network is scheduled by 1990 and for the subscriber network by 1992.

7.3   INTERNATIONAL TRUNK SYSTEMS

Fiber optic (especially single-mode with its greater distances between repeaters) is certainly an economically attractive alternative to metallic cable, and even to satellite for intercontinental and long overland routes. Internationally, projects having individual values in the tens of hundreds of millions of dollars ranges have been completed or are in prospect.

Within Europe, West Germany and East Germany have reached a cooperative agreement for an optical-fiber link to extend 220 km inside East Germany (March 1985). The cost involved is $15 million and the link will accommodate 30 000 telephone channels. Another example is furnished by the UK company STC plc which has obtained contracts for fiber-optic trunk installations within Denmark.

Contracts totalling US $335 million to supply and lay TAT-8, the first transatlantic communications cable to use optical fibers, were signed on 12 July 1984. This new cable is now in place and should meet the growth in demand for transatlantic communications for a few years. The Intelsat V satellite communications system came into service in 1981 and Intelsat VI is due for launch as soon as launch vehicle availability allows. At least until the early 1990s there will remain an approximately equal division of telephone channels provided by satellite and cable.

The full-load capacity of TAT-8 approaches 40 000 equivalent simultaneous telephone calls, which is three times greater than the combined traffic capacity of all the other transatlantic cables. An ocean-floor junction box represents a unique aspect of this project. This junction box is located just off the European continental shelf and it serves to branch the cable to both England and France.

Contracts for the construction of TAT-8 were placed with AT & T Communications for the section from the USA to the branch, with STC for the section from the junction to the UK and with CIT/Alcatel and Cables de Lyons for the section from the junction box to France.

STC implemented the 520 km segment from the junction box to the UK landing point in Widemouth Bay, Cornwall, under a contract worth $71 million. The French, under a contract worth $44 million, will make the 310 km segment from the junction to Penmarch on the Brittany coast.

AT & T supplied the 580 km segment from Tuckerton, New Jersey, to the junction box, and also coordinated the activities of the three suppliers. AT & T's contract was worth US $249 million. A total of 29 PTTs in Europe and North America are co-owners of TAT-8, their investments being in proportion to their anticipated ultilization of the system. AT & T Communications has the largest share, 37%, worth $123 million.

The system comprises two working pairs of single-mode fibers, each driven by 1300 nm lasers operating at 296 Mbit/s. One working pair links the USA and UK, the other the USA and France. A third pair of single-mode fibers act as a standby for the main crossing.

In common with all trunk fiber-optic systems the fibers are all *spliced* at drum-to-drum intervals and into the repeater units.

TAT-8's system life is 25 years (two-and-a-half times that of a satellite system) and fault regulations stipulate a maximum of three component failures during this period. However, technology is progressing so rapidly in this field that obsolescence usually arrives before the end of a system's nominal life. TAT-1, for example, which was installed in 1956, was taken out of service in the early 1980s. It could only handle 50 telephone circuits. When TAT-7 (metallic cable) came into operation in 1983 a total of 11 200 cable circuits were provided between Europe and North America.

Operation of TAT-8 at 296 Mbit/s is equivalent to a basic capacity of 7500 telephone channels. However, digital multiplexing equipment would increase this to 37 800 channels, this equipment being introduced as required. The system includes 125 repeaters, spaced at an average distance of 57 km.

The number of telephone calls between the UK and the USA grew at almost 30% per annum throughout the 1970s and is, through the late 1980s and early 1990s, estimated to be doubling every five years or so. At present about 60 million *telephone* calls are made each year between the two countries, divided about equally between satellite and cable.

There also exists (recently inaugurated) a $396 million fiber-optic cable contract to link Singapore to Indonesia, Sri Lanka, Djibouti, Saudi Arabia, Egypt, Italy and France. In June 1986 the telecommunications utilities of Japan, South Korea and Hong Kong agreed to the construction of a submarine fiber cable that will link Hong Kong, Seoul and Tokyo. The total cost of the project is $200 million and this system will interconnect with other trans-Pacific links including those to the USA. It is expected that the system will become operational around 1990, but it will not be extended to Singapore until the 1990s.

Contracts worth a total of approximately $200 million have been let for a second transatlantic link (TAT-9) with a 1991 completion date. This system will operate at 565 Mbit/s (almost double that of TAT-8) and includes spurs extending to Italy, Palma in Majorca and Marseille in Southern France. The companies in the consortium for this are: British Telecom, France Telecom, Telefonica of Spain, AT & T,

Teleglobe of Canada and Italcable of Italy for the Mediterranean section. Further increases in demand have led to the requirement for a third cable, TAV-1, which is expected to be in service before the end of 1989. TAV-1 will provide connections between the Eastern seaboard of the USA, Northern Spain, Brittany and the UK. TAT-9 and TAV-1 will also have spurs to Eastern Canada.

Licences have also been issued by USA and UK authorities to let contracts, implement, land and operate 'PTAT-1', the first privately owned transatlantic system, again using fiber-optic cables. With PTAT-1 also due to be cut-over during 1989 a successor, PTAT-2, is planned for 1992 completion.

The Mediterranean region is also to be served by a fiber-optic transmission network known as EMOS (Euro-Mediterranean Optical System). With Palermo in Sicily as the hub for Mediterranean systems a future connection to Alexandria is planned, allowing connection to the Middle East and to South East Asia (Fig. 7.1).

In fact, the first South East link, known as 'SEA–ME–WE', is due to

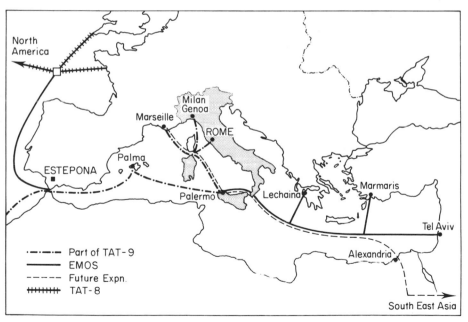

Fig. 7.1 Proposed Mediterranean fiber cable transmission network, and other related planned connections (with grateful acknowledgment to the editors of *Communications Engineering International*, May, 1987, from which this figure was taken with their permission).

be cut-over by the end of 1990, connecting the Middle East to Sri Lanka, Singapore and Papua. Pacific plans are indicated as follows:

Hong Kong/Japan/Korea (H-J-K)   1990
Seattle/Hawaii (HAW-4)   1989
Vancouver/Tokyo (PPAC)   1989
Hawaii/Japan (TPC-3)   1989
Philippines–TPC-3 link (CP-2)   1989
Sydney/Auckland (TASMAN-2)   1991
Sydney/Asia   1995
Auckland/USA   1993

There are plans for fiber-cable installations in the Gulf region. Bahrain will almost certainly represent the hub of any new system and a 520 km submarine fiber link is due to be installed between that country and Kuwait (Cable & Wireless have a 40% stake in Bahrain's PTT: Batelco). Actual implementation will depend upon a lasting peace in the area.

The total value of all trunk fiber-optic systems worldwide will approach $5 billion by 1994.

8

Instrumentation

8.1 BIT ERROR RATE

Electronic tests can readily be performed on the transmitter and the receiver of almost *any* link of most types of communication system, usually employing an oscilloscope, a logic analyzer or a signal analyzer (a notable exception being the satellite itself in a satellite communication system). The modulation of the transmitter and signal recovery at the receiver are conventionally checked in this manner. These types of tests are performed in the electrical environment of otherwise optical systems.

Bit error rate (BER) measurements may be carried out on conveniently short fiber links, but with the signal level deliberately reduced to artificially increase the error rate to exceptionally high values (since BER rises as signal-to-noise ratio falls, as outlined in Chapter 1). This procedure is, however mathematically rather elaborate, because the normal operating BER must be indirectly evaluated.

Optical variable attenuators, available commercially from companies such as Anritsu, are valuable in this type of work. However, BER can be measured (given sufficient hours or days) with a more direct technique involving a word pattern generator and an error detector.

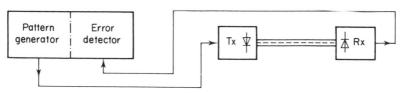

Fig. 8.1 A scheme for the measurement of bit error rate (BER) in a digital communications system.

A suitable arrangement for this is shown in Fig. 8.1. Firms such as Hewlett-Packard supply combined pattern generator/error detector units.

For LANs and most other data networks the BER should be kept below 10^{-9}. In some very high quality links it has to be as low as 10^{-12} or even lower.

8.2 OPTICAL POWER AND ATTENUATION

Optical power measurements are simply and regularly obtainable using pocket-size calibrated instruments. The optical/electronic converter is normally 'remote' from the instrument itself, being connected by a length of electrical cable. Care must be taken over compatibility of connectors to the converter; either the manufacturer provides calibrated adaptors for the user's systems, or the user himself must overcome the problem.

Minimum receiver power input levels can be checked. Differences between powers (dBm) give attenuation results in dB, e.g. the loss along a specific section of cable and power levels down to the nanowatt region can be measured. Companies such as Anritsu and Solartron Instruments supply suitable instruments. Current versions of such instruments enable measurements to be made on single-mode fiber links operating at 1550 nm and typically provide about 70 dB dynamic range.

8.3 OPTICAL TIME-DOMAIN REFLECTOMETERS (OTDRs)

8.3.1 Basic principle

The optical time-domain reflectometer (OTDR) is now an established instrument with which to characterize a fiber's attenuation, uniformity, splice loss, breaks and lengths. Even dispersion can be measured with a suitable, short-pulse-width OTDR. Its main advantage is one-port operation at the fiber input with no need to access the fiber output, i.e. 'everything happens' at the input port to the cable. The basic scheme is shown in Fig. 8.2.

A pulse generator drives a laser diode which then launches high-power optical pulses (100 mW to several watts) into the fiber. Pulse widths are from 5 to 100 ns and repetition rates are a few kilohertz.

The signal returning from the fiber is separated from the launched signal by a directional coupler in the form of a beam splitter (as shown in Fig. 8.2) or any other appropriate coupler technology.

An APD detects the returned signal which is then 'averaged', amplified and fed to the vertical amplifier of an oscilloscope. The result is a display of one-way optical loss as a function of fiber lengths or, alternatively, round-trip time.

Backscatter and reflections are readily identified as shown in Fig. 8.3 which provides an example for a 4 km total fiber length. Three fiber

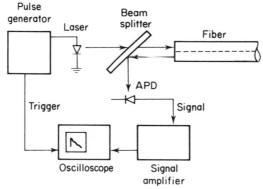

Fig. 8.2 Schematic diagram showing the operating principle of an optical time-domain reflectometer (OTDR).

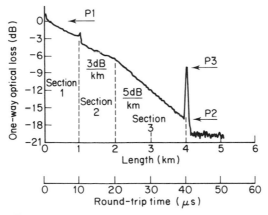

Fig. 8.3 A representative OTDR display.

sections spliced together, can be identified:

● two 1-km long sections (1 and 2), followed by
● one 2-km long section (3).

A reflection and corresponding splice loss of 0.6 dB (rather poor) is evident between sections 1 and 2. The splice loss between 2 and 3 is sufficiently small to be unobservable on this scale.

Distances can typically be gauged to at least 20 km and the resolution is typically 1 meter on these types of instruments.

Noise is a problem in measuring long lengths by OTDR. For unambiguous end detection, point P3 in the return must be clearly distinguishable from the noise.

8.3.2   More advanced features and commercially available instruments

Instead of launching single optical pulses with large amplitude, a more recent OTDR technique uses pseudo-random bit (PRB) patterns at the fiber input, to increase the total amount of power in the fiber and hence to obtain a larger reflected signal. With PRB correlation must be used in the signal analysis. Some specification details of a selection of OTDRs are summarized in Table 8.1.

Several manufacturers offer single-mode as well as multimode cable test facilities, with dispersion measurement options. It is worth noting that in some cases the 1300/1550 nm models enable a rather greater range to be reached (low-loss window). But this is far from generally true; Anritsu's 850 nm model reaches 72 km and Biddle Instruments make a 830-nm instrument reaching 50 km. Hewlett-Packard claim that their model HP 8145A will allow meaningful measurement to be conducted as far out as 200 km.

A further offering comes from Schlumberger Instruments, whose '7721' OTDR operates at either 1300 or 1550 nm as desired and is claimed 'can fully qualify a 30 km optical link within 2 minutes'.

Other manufacturers of OTDRs include:

● Advantest
● Ando Corporation
● Hewlett-Packard
● Photodyne

Table 8.1 Examples of some commercially available OTDRs and their characteristics *

Manufacturer	Model	Wavelength (nm)	Amplitude resolution (dB)	Distance resolution (m)	Distance measurement accuracy (%)	Maximum distance range (km)	One-way backscatter dynamic range (dB)
Anritsu (1300 nm and 1550 nm also available)	MW98A/MH913B	850	0.01	1	—	144	—
Cossor Electronics	OFL 119 and	904	0.1	±20	±1	30	—
	OFL 213	1300	—	±20 (full range)	—	31	20
	OFL 215 (for SM)	1550	0.05	±10	±0.1	42	17
Laser Precision Corp (820 nm also available)	TD-9940	1300	0.027	1	±0.01	13%	—
Orionics Inc (820 nm also available)	SCD-202/OTD-11?	1300	±0.1	1	±1	20	—
STC Defence Systems Ltd	OR 3-905 and	905 and	—	±4	—	15	20
	OR 3-850	850					
	OR 6	1300	—	—	—	—	—
	OR 7 (high resolution)	—	—	±0.05	—	5	—
Tektronix (820 nm also available 19.9 km range)	OF-152	1300	±0.05	1	±0.3	60	—
	OF-235 (SM)	1300/1550	—	—	—	100	—

* Other performance characteristics are also required for the intending user (see notes on OTDR specifications)

- Siecor
- Wilcom Products, and
- York Technology.

(There are a number of others and the situation changes frequently.)

Unit prices vary considerably, ranging from about $3000 to around $55 000 depending upon the sophistication demanded and the facilities required.

In some cases real-time measurement results are needed so that a cable splice can be adjusted for minimum attenuation. Other users need display on a CRT screen and in some instances a print-out on 'hard-copy' (usually chart-recorder paper) is desired. Some manufacturers offer 1550 nm OTDRs and at least nine manufacturers will supply switched 1300/1550 nm instruments.

All (or most by far) of the OTDR manufacturers offer products covering the *long-haul* market, generally defined as 'upwards of some tens of kilometers'. This may be because short-to-medium haul, LAN and MAN, applications are not necessarily best served by OTDRs. For many of these more localized test and check time-sensitive networks relatively unsophisticated testers such as attenuation test sets (e.g. Fotec's) or optical power meters are often quite sufficient for the purpose.

8.3.3 Some notes regarding OTDR specifications

There are dangers in interpreting aspects of OTDR specifications and therefore some cautionary notes are presented here.

Instrument choice depends upon a *combination* of factors, notably

(i)   *useful* distance range;
(ii) OTDR *system* amplitude resolution (*not* display resolution);
(iii) pulse width and averaging times used;
(iv) portability and ease of use;
(v)   reliability;
(vi) as usual, the 'bottom line', i.e. unit price.

More detailed points include the following:

Distance range: It is all very well having, say 100 km ultimate capability, but often it is the OTDR *sensitivity* that may limit the useful range to 30 or 40 km.

Amplitude resolution:

- Some instruments have *display* resolutions as fine as 0.01 dB, *but* the received signal-to-noise power ratio obtainable must enable this to be useful, often not the case.
- OTDRs can only give a rough estimate of splice loss (because any two spliced fibers have what are known as 'differing Rayleigh scattering coefficients' and also the average loss is being measured in two directions through the fiber outward and return).

9

Current trends and forthcoming developments

9.1 THE POTENTIAL OF FIBER OPTICS

The fiber optics industry is still in its infancy. There can be little doubt that fiber will in time — in particular during the 1990s — begin to penetrate; the subscriber loop, data buses in cars, industrial communications, further financial service centers and further military applications.

The subscriber loop will probably start with the business sector, then steadily shift to domestic customers also. Not all of the systems will use silica fiber: some may well employ the polymer fibers under development. A 100-m length of polymer fiber typically provides a bandwidth approaching 250 MHz, which is ample for wideband subscriber 'final link' services. Such fibers, however, have to be operated at 660 nm and LEDs at this (visible red) wavelength only have an available bandwidth of about 20 MHz. So the limitation is in the LED transmitting device. One advantage of operating at 660 nm is the visibility of the light — it is possible to actually see the light transmission (or indeed therefore any break in this transmission). Such polymer systems may be used in cars and other road vehicles for data signals.

To date, practical systems have hardly begun to tap the potential of fiber in terms of available bandwidth. The chart given as Fig. 9.1 indicates bit-rate capabilities for several types of information transmission systems.

Although 'coax' is shown to have several Gbit/s capability it is of course very restricted in terms of distance between repeaters, as described in Chapter 2. It is noteworthy that fiber (single-mode) can

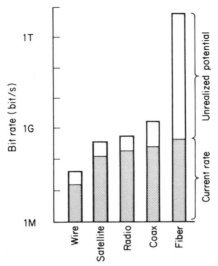

Fig. 9.1 Maximum achievable bit rates associated with a variety of transmission media (with grateful acknowledgment to the editors of *Communications Engineering International*, March, 1987, from which this figure was taken with their permission).

potentially be operated at bit rates up to several hundred terabits per second (Tbit/s), although realizing this would require as yet unrealized coherent all-optical processing. Such bit rates imply the equivalent of ten billion simultaneous 64 Kbit/s telephone channels.

Only *coherent techniques*, covered briefly in the last part of this chapter, will enable at least some of the unrealized potential to be tapped, probably only with trunk systems at first.

9.2   THIRD GENERATION LANs, MANs AND WANs

As described in Chapter 6 we may think generally in terms of three generations of LANs, differentiated by classes of serial operating bit rates.

Third-generation operation is characterized by bit rates of some hundreds of Mbit/s, up towards and beyond 1000 Mbit/s (i.e. 1 Gbit/s). Such systems are presently the province of R & D activities but they will allow very-high-speed interactive computing with the addition of real-time color video. For example, the University of

Gothenberg in Sweden currently have a 3 Gbit/s ring-topology LAN operating using a laser and single-mode fiber.

These types of systems, operating over distances amounting to several kilometers between nodes of a network, demand optical fiber interconnections because of the (bandwidth) × (range) products required. Networks of the 1990s and beyond will almost certainly increasingly use such systems.

MANs, carrying mixed speech, video, cable TV and data will need to bridge out to other networks and routes such as national or international networks (at the higher levels) or private data networks which will usually be localized. Increased information flow requirements are already resulting in bottlenecks in such systems and fiber provides an obvious solution.

WANs, operating at these speeds or higher, will in some instances be formed as self-contained systems. In other installations WANs will essentially comprise groups of interconnected LANs or MANs.

9.3 OPTOELECTRONIC INTEGRATED CIRCUITS

With 'conventional' electronics we are well used to the concept of integrated circuits: ICs or microchips.

It is relatively straightforward to consider a number of optoelectronic devices integrated, at least in hybrid form, on the same microchip as many other components. Indeed, integrated optoelectronic couplers have been available for many years (firms like Texas Instruments have been pre-eminent in this respect). So, the hybrid integration of LEDs, lasers, PIN and APD detectors is fully practicable today, although APDs are rather more difficult to integrate due to the higher voltages (see Chapter 4). Several firms manufacture integrated optoelectronic products such as:

- lasers integrated with transistors,
- fiber-optic transmitters,
- integrated optoelectronic repeaters,
- optoelectronic transceivers incorporating data processing chips (TTL, ECL, GaAs).

Firms such as Plessey have already designed and introduced integrated optoelectronic PIN-FET receivers to operate at 565 Mbit/s (avalanche detectors are necessary at still higher bit rates).

Gallium arsenide (GaAs) monolithic electronic IC technology increasingly impacts the high-speed scene on a commercial basis — both for digital microchips and microwave analog integrated circuits. These gallium arsenide chips are required in several other modern communications systems including: earth-based receivers for satellite communications and some radars — notably those using the phased arrays — briefly described later. Most of these applications involve analog chips but digital gallium arsenide integrated circuits (microchips) represent a strong contender for fifth generation computer hardware or any high-speed digital systems. Firms who are active in the development of these chips include: Plessey, Rockwell International, Harris Semiconductor, Fujitsu and Thomson-CSF (there are many others.)

With optoelectronic products designed for fiber-optics applications advantage is increasingly taken of the materials/processing/manufacture broad compatibility of GaAs electronics and GaAs-based 'photonics'. Lasers, LEDs and receiving devices are also generally based upon GaAs technology, with additional materials requirements such as aluminum in these devices.

Entirely optical (photonic) integrated circuits represent the next generation of chips.

Passive structures, the couplers and WDM products manufactured, for example, by Corning-France (see Chapter 3) are among the first examples of photonic ICs. Active photonic ICs are under development in a number of laboratories worldwide, for example, AT & T Bell, Plessey, NEC and Thomson-CSF.

9.4 SWITCHED FIBER SYSTEMS AND OPTICAL SWITCHES

Several organizations have shown considerable interest in packet switches capable of switching voice, video and data signals and allocating bandwidth dynamically to subscribers at bit rates up to, typically, 280 Mbit/s.

CNET (France) have demonstrated such a system experimentally using the technique of asynchronous time-division multiplexing (ATDM). This label-switched system is known as 'Prelude'. The switching is performed electronically (at bit rates as high as 4.6 Gbit/s) and an optimum combination of metallic cable and fiber is used. The

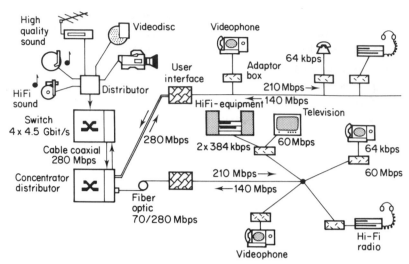

Fig. 9.2 Demonstrated capabilities of CNET's 'Prelude' packet-switched system (with grateful acknowledgment to the editors of *Communication Systems Worldwide*, April, 1987, from which this figure was taken with their permission).

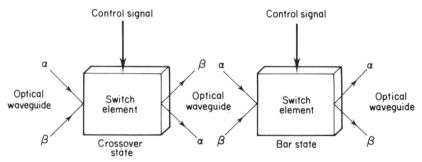

Fig. 9.3 Basic structure of an all-optical switching element (with grateful acknowledgment to the editors of *Telecommunications*, May, 1987, from which this figure was taken with their permission).

capabilities and structure of Prelude are indicated in Fig. 9.2 where the variety of services offered is also shown.

Although this ATDM has the backing of Alcatel, NEC and AT & T (and was led by an EC 'Race' project), its future is by no means assured because it requires substantial overall European commitment.

Entirely optical switches (as far as signal paths are concerned) often use chip materials such as lithium niobate to achieve their functions. A basic switching element is shown in Fig. 9.3, while crossover and directional coupler switches are shown in Fig. 9.4.

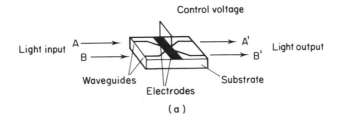

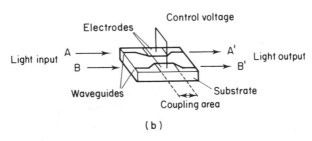

Fig. 9.4   An all-optical crossover switch (a) and a coupler switch (b) (with grateful acknowledgment to the editors of *Telecommunications*, May, 1987, from which this figure was taken with their permission).

The details of operation are beyond the scope of this text.

Ericsson of Sweden have developed an 8 × 8 optical non-blocking switch matrix produced on a single chip of lithium niobate and containing an array of 64 switch points. Such devices have strategic importance for future all-phototronic PABXs, or 'LAN-like', switching systems (third generation and beyond).

Other organizations who are active in this field include those mentioned in Section 9.3.

Thomson are studying optical beam steering using holographic diffraction gratings.

9.5   EXTREMELY NARROW LINE-WIDTH LASERS AND COHERENT SYSTEMS

Laboratories such as those of British Telecom and Fujitsu regularly announce the achievement of semiconductor lasers with ever-narrower line widths. Products having these levels of specifications will be essential for use in *coherent systems* which require line widths of the order of a few kilohertz. Such line widths are technically feasible. Most

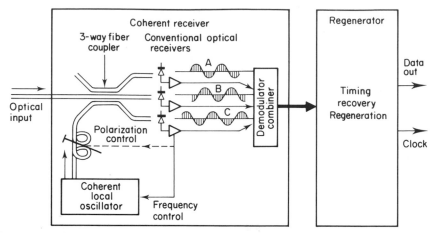

Fig. 9.5 Schematic diagram of STC's (UK) coherent optical receiver (with grateful acknowledgment to the editors of *Communications Engineering International*, March, 1987, from which this figure was taken with their permission).

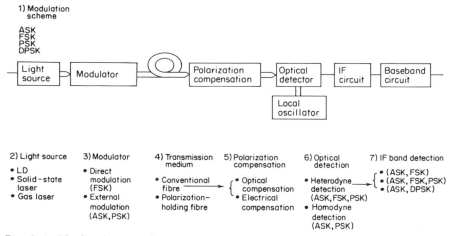

Fig. 9.6 Block schematic diagram indicating possible options for coherent optical transmission systems (with grateful acknowledgment to the editors of *Telecommunications*, June, 1988, from which this figure was taken with their permission).

current coherent systems research centers on the use of relatively large, and ultimately inappropriate gas lasers.

Other requirements for semiconductor lasers in advanced systems include: electronic (or optical) tunability and compatibility with WDM.

The coherent systems implications of availability of these lasers include the following improvements:

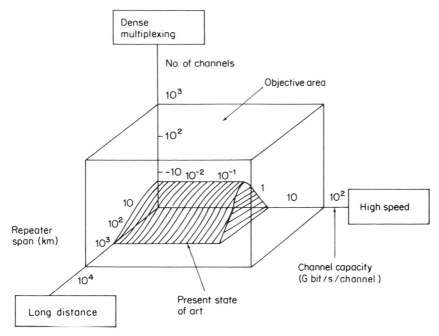

Fig. 9.7 Research targets for coherent optical communications technology (with grateful acknowledgment to the editors of *Telecommunications*, June, 1988, from which this figure was taken with their permission).

- multichannel WDM (24 GHz of bandwidth is available within the 1550 nm window);
- receiver sensitivity can be improved by up to 20 dB (hence greater repeater/regenerator spacings — up to 180 km at least).

Special designs of receivers are required in coherent optical systems and an example of a phase-sensitive receiver is shown in Fig. 9.5.

In this system the 'coherent local oscillator' is a very narrow line-width semiconductor laser such as a distributed feedback laser.

These types of techniques could be utilized in cable TV and other subscriber networks using FDM, selecting channels by tuning to a local optical frequency.

Regarding coherent *trunk* systems, AT & T Bell, for example, have demonstrated the transmission of information at 2 Gbit/s over 170 km of unrepeated single-mode fiber. A block diagram indicating the layout and possible options for such coherent transmission systems is given in Fig. 9.6.

These approaches to future systems are of such importance that many professional groups are actively working on related techniques and technologies that could extend communication capabilities dramatically using, where possible, existing cables containing single-mode fibers. Research targets in this area are indicated in Fig. 9.7, where the cube represents the future target whilst the shaded volume represents the current state-of-the-art.

9.6 MICROWAVE TRANSMISSION AND APPLICATIONS, AND 'PHASED-ARRAY' RADARS

Microwave signals can be used to modulate semiconductor lasers which then transfer their light, at GHz bandwidths, on to optical fibers. Applications are important for this type of technique, ranging from satellite signal transmission — on Earth or in a spacecraft — to signal transfer in special new forms of radars known as phased arrays. In these radars the antennas are electronically scanned rather than physically moved and it has been demonstrated that single-mode fibers will effectively transfer microwave signals to and from elements in these phased arrays. Important advantages include the absence of EMI and the complete preservation of relative phase. Bandwidths at least as high as 20 GHz are available for microwaves over single-mode fiber.

9.7 ULTRA-LOW-LOSS LONG-WAVELENGTH TRANSMISSION

Most of this text, by far, concentrates on electro-optics operating at wavelengths below 1600 nm.

There are, however, some special materials which may prove suitable for fibers and which exhibit extremely low optical losses at wavelengths within the range extending from 5000 to 10 000 nm. Losses in these special materials can be as low as 0.01 dB/km, or less, which should be contrasted with the values normally associated with silica fibers. Remember that the lowest possible attenuation or loss in silica fiber is about 0.16 dB/km.

The availability of such fibers would mean that we could have a fiber cable 300 km long before just half the input power was lost. But it should be appreciated that *splice losses* would then almost certainly dominate unless extremely long uninterrupted runs become feasible.

Practical links would be many hundreds, or even thousands of kilometers long, with no repeaters between transmitter and receiver. It is, however, true that we would still have significant dispersion and these special fiber materials are more difficult to handle than silica fiber (some involve toxic processes).

Sources (LEDs and lasers) which operate in the 7000 to 15 000 nm range are currently being studied, although they require quite complex semiconductors for their operation.

Modulation rates beyond 20 Gbit/s (20 000 Mbit/s) are possible and these sources will be integrated as explained in Section 9.3.

9.8 SOLITONS

A soliton is a continuous wave or a pulse which does not lose its shape as it travels through a particular medium. A familiar example is a water wave travelling down a channel (e.g. a canal). Indeed, solitons were discovered about 100 years ago and their significance for future fiber-optic systems has only been appreciated comparatively recently.

In 1988 Bell Laboratories succeeded in transmitting soliton light pulses for a distance of about 4000 km around a fiber loop without any electrical regeneration. A soliton having 0.4 ps duration could theoretically be used to transmit data at 2000 Gbit/s, i.e. with 4000 times the capacity of the existing 565 Mbit/s trunk systems.

Glossary of terms and abbreviations

Absorption loss Attenuation of the optical signal within the fiber-optic transmission medium. Usually specified in terms of dB/km.

Acceptance angle The maximum angle at which a light ray may be incident upon a fiber core and accepted for transmission. This is a property of the fiber and is dependent on the indices of refraction of the core and cladding material.

APD Avalanche photodiode. A type of (semiconductor) photodetecting diode that depends for its operation on electrons which are multiplied by incident photons. APDs are used mainly in high-sensitivity, long-range and high-speed systems.

Bandwidth The total range of frequencies needed to send some specified information at a given rate. Telephone speech (one 'channel') needs only a few kilohertz, kHz, of bandwidth. Just one channel of television demands at least several MHz. *The greater the amount of information and/or the greater its necessary transfer rate the larger the bandwidth required.*

Bit Short for *bin*ary digi*t*; fundamental unit of amount of information. A bit can only be a '1' or a '0'.

Bit rate (or information rate, or data rate, or 'channel capacity'). This is of great importance in communication systems. The units are bits per second (bit/s). We often meet Kbit/s and Mbit/s. This information rate is the minimum speed at which some specified information must be sent for satisfactory reception.

Bit error rate (BER) The probability (for any receiver) of actually receiving a bit in error. Highly dependent on system design and link budget.

CATV (Cable TV or Community Antenna TV). Many thousands or more subscribers served from a tapped usually metallic (coax.) cable system, itself fed by a single receiving antenna (the 'community' antenna). Several networks now use at least some fiber.

CCTV (Closed-Circuit TV). TV without broadcast (transmit or receive), and most often monochrome with lower definition than the more familiar broadcast. Best known perhaps in monitoring and in shop or bank security systems. Clearly, small cameras, cabling and monitors (TVs) are required (note that optical fiber cables are tougher than metal ones and are inherently secure).

Cladding The covering material which encases the core of an optical fiber. The cladding material is always of a lower index of refraction than the core material and may be either silica or plastic.

Core The center dielectric in an optical fiber through which the optical wave propagates. This material is usually silica and it has a higher index of refraction than the cladding material.

Decibels, dB Simply ten times the logarithm of a ratio of two powers, P_1 and P_2 say: $10 \log (P_2/P_1)$dB.
Very useful in the design, implementation and assessment of communication systems. We add dB where we have amplifiers (gain) and subtract where we have cables, etc (losses). An important example is '3 dB', which refers to a (linear) power ratio factor of 2.

dBm Power units obtained by referring the amount of power to one milliwatt (mW), 1×10^{-3}W. Thus 2μW are equivalent to: $10 \log (2 \times 10^{-6}/1 \times 10^{-3})$ or -27 dBm.

Dispersion In optical fibers, fundamental material, modal and 'waveguide' mechanisms leading to signal delay. With digital systems the main consequence is pulse-spreading. Dispersion can be cancelled to zero in single-mode fibers but with multimode it often imposes the *system design limit*. (Usual units are ns/km.)

FET Field-effect transistor. May be in silicon or gallium arsenide (GaAs FET). Often used in conjunction with PIN-FET photodetectors for fiber-optic receiver 'front-ends'.

Frequency The regular repetition rate of a carrier (or a clock pulse sequence in a digital system). Frequencies are expressed in Hz, with more familiar multiple units being kHz, MHz or GHz.

Graded index fiber An optical fiber whose index of refraction is a function of the radial distance from the fiber's axis. This type of fiber does not depend on interfacial reflection; it uses the index gradient to refocus the rays within the core. It generally exhibits higher bandwidth than 'step' index multimode fibers.

Injection laser diode (ILD) A solid-state semiconductor device consisting of at least one $p-n$ junction capable of emitting coherent or stimulated radiation under specified conditions. The device will have incorporated into its structure a resonant optical cavity. Generally known simply as a 'laser diode'.

LANs (Local-Area Networks). A controlled set of interconnections between a number of computer terminals, spread around a 'local' or 'limited' area, usually within the same building or a close group of buildings.

Linewidth (or spectral bandwidth). The linewidth or spectral bandwidth for single peak devices is the difference between the wavelengths at which the radiant intensity is 50% (unless otherwise stated) of the maximum value.

MANs (Metropolitan Area Networks). As their name implies, networks, covering towns, or cities, or substantial parts thereof. MANs may be more or less self-contained or may interconnect to LANs or to other external networks via 'gateways'.

Modulation The process of impressing the signal, which we desire to send, on to the carrier which is used so that the signal is transmitted in an effective manner. Techniques include amplitude modulation (AM), frequency modulation (FM) as analog approaches and amplitude-shift keying (ASK) as a digital approach. FM, and also ASK, are often used in fiber-optic systems.

Multiplexing The combination of several information signals from different channels into a single channel for transmission; frequency-division multiplexing (FDM), time-division multiplexing (TDM), and optical wavelength-division multiplexing (WDM).

Multimode fiber Optical fibers with relatively large core diameters compared to single-mode fibers. The core diameter of multimode fibers can range from 25 to 200 microns.

Noise In general, any unwanted electrical disturbances. A lot of background noise is almost continuous and very broad band. Some noise comes in bursts. In fiber optics it includes unwanted background light and inherent electronic effects in the receivers. We specify a minimum signal-to-noise power ratio for a receiver: S/N where S is average signal power and N is average noise power (W, mW, μW, nW). Thus S/N must usually well exceed 1.0 and quite often exceed 10. *Noise is a big problem in receiver design and use.*

Numerical aperture (NA). A number which defines the light-gathering capability of a specific fiber. The numerical aperture is equal to the sine of the maximum acceptance angle (qv).

PIN A commonly encountered semiconductor photodetecting diode. Suitable for fiber-optic receivers in short-to-medium range systems, operating at low-to-moderate frequencies (slow/moderate bit rates).

Refractive index The ratio of the velocity of light in a vacuum to its velocity in the core or cladding of a fiber.

Responsivity The term used to describe the static 'sensitivity' of the photodetector. It is the ratio of the output current or voltage to the input optical power in watts. When responsivity is indicated at a particular wavelength (in amperes/watt), it denotes the spectral response of the device.

Signal-to-noise ratio (see under Noise).

Single-mode fiber An optical fiber with a very small core diameter (usually in the range of 2–10 microns). Such fibers are normally used only with laser sources due to their very small acceptance core. Since the core diameter approaches the wavelength of the source, only a single mode is propagated.

Speed (v) All radio and light waves travel at nearly 300 000 km per second in air or space. This speed is nearly always simply abbreviated c.

In materials like plastics, silica, etc (used in optical fibers) the waves travel more slowly; it is about halved in silica, giving 150 000 km per second.

Step-index fiber An optical fiber which has a core and a cladding with an abrupt change in the refractive index at the core–cladding interface. The index of the cladding is usually less than the core index to permit total internal reflection. Single-mode fiber is the most obvious example of step index.

VANS (Value-Added Network Services). Arrangements which enable companies to make use of an existing physical network, usually a national PTT's telephone network, to provide various types of services (at a profit) to third parties. Essentially this adds value to the physical network.

WANs (Wide-Area Networks). Larger in scale than LANs, WANs often extend over some tens or hundreds of km. They frequently use graded-index multimode, or single-mode, fibers and may comprise a set of interconnected LANs.

Waveform The variation of an electrical (e.g. voltage) or optical (usually power) quantity with time.

Wavelength (λ) The distance (m, nm), travelled by a wave during its own period. Since the period is $1/f$ where f is the frequency, the wavelength must be $\lambda = v/f$ where v is the speed. With fiber optics the wavelength often lies somewhere in the range 600 to 1600 nm.

Index